Data Mining: Tools, Techniques, Frameworks and Applications

Data Mining: Tools, Techniques, Frameworks and Applications

Edited by **Mick Benson**

New York

Published by Willford Press,
118-35 Queens Blvd., Suite 400,
Forest Hills, NY 11375, USA
www.willfordpress.com

Data Mining: Tools, Techniques, Frameworks and Applications
Edited by Mick Benson

International Standard Book Number: 978-1-68285-000-8 (Hardback)

Printed in the United States of America.

Contents

Preface

Data mining is an important branch of computer science and information technology management that deals with the discovery and analysis of datasets. This book covers in detail some existent theories as well as innovative concepts revolving around data mining such as bio data analytics, analysis of social structures and patterns, correlations and fluctuations, etc. With its detailed analyses and data, this book will prove immensely beneficial to professionals and students involved in this area at various levels.

This book unites the global concepts and researches in an organized manner for a comprehensive understanding of the subject. It is a ripe text for all researchers, students, scientists or anyone else who is interested in acquiring a better knowledge of this dynamic field.

I extend my sincere thanks to the contributors for such eloquent research chapters. Finally, I thank my family for being a source of support and help.

Editor

A large-scale community structure analysis in Facebook

Emilio Ferrara[*]

[*]Correspondence:
ferrarae@indiana.edu
Center for Complex Networks and
Systems Research, School of
Informatics and Computing, Indiana
University, Bloomington, USA
Department of Mathematics and
Informatics, University of Messina,
Messina, Italy

Abstract

Understanding social dynamics that govern human phenomena, such as communications and social relationships is a major problem in current *computational social sciences*. In particular, given the unprecedented success of *online social networks* (OSNs), in this paper we are concerned with the analysis of aggregation patterns and social dynamics occurring among users of the largest OSN as the date: Facebook. In detail, we discuss the mesoscopic features of the community structure of this network, considering the perspective of the communities, which has not yet been studied on such a large scale. To this purpose, we acquired a sample of this network containing millions of users and their social relationships; then, we unveiled the communities representing the aggregation units among which users gather and interact; finally, we analyzed the statistical features of such a network of communities, discovering and characterizing some specific organization patterns followed by individuals interacting in online social networks, that emerge considering different sampling techniques and clustering methodologies. This study provides some clues of the tendency of individuals to establish social interactions in online social networks that eventually contribute to building a well-connected social structure, and opens space for further social studies.

Introduction

Social media and online social networks (OSNs) represent a revolution in Web users behavior that is spreading at an unprecedented rate during the latest years. Online users aggregate on platforms such as Facebook and Twitter creating large social networks of millions of persons that interact and group each other. People create social ties constituting groups based on existing relationships in real life, such as on relatives, friends, colleagues, or based on common interests, shared tastes, *etc.*

In the context of *computational social sciences*, the analysis of social dynamics, including the description of those unique features that characterize online social networks, is acquiring an increasing importance in current literature [1–3].

One of the challenges for *network scientists* is to provide techniques to collect [4] and process [5] data from online social networks in an automatic fashion, and strategies to unveil the features that characterize these types of complex networks [6]. In addition, these methods should be capable of working in such large-scale scenarios [7].

Amongst all the relevant problems in this area, the analysis of the so-called *community structure* of online social networks acquired relevant attention during latest years [8–14]. Recently, several relevant quantitative works have been presented to this purpose [15–19].

Studying the community structure of a network helps in explaining social dynamics of interaction among groups of individuals [20–22], but also to quantitatively investigate social theories such as Milgram's *small world* [23], Granovetter's *strength of weak ties* [24], Borgatti's and Everett's *core-periphery structure* [25, 26], and so forth.

Furthermore, discovering and analyzing the community structure is a topic of great interest for its economical and marketing implications [27]. For example, it could be possible to improve the advertising performance by identifying and targeting the most influential users of each community, exploiting effects such as the *word-of-mouth* and the spread of information within the community itself [28]. Similarly, exploiting the affiliations of users to communities might be effective to provide them useful recommendations on the base of common interests shared with their friends [29].

Finally, the community detection problem has plenty of challenges from a computational perspective, since it is highly related to the problem of clustering large, possibly heterogeneous, datasets [30–35].

In this work we are concerned with the analysis of the community structure of the largest online social network as to date: Facebook. In particular, we acquire a sample from the Facebook social graph (*i.e.*, the network of relationships among the users), and then we apply two different state-of-the-art algorithms to unveil its underlying community structure (see the Appendix for technical details).

The further analysis of the mesoscopic features of this network puts into evidence the organization patterns that describe the connectivity of users in large online social network.

To summarize, in the remainder of the paper we will discuss the following results:

(i) The emergence of a tendency of social network users at the formation of communities of heterogeneous size (following a heavy-tailed distribution), which means that there exist several groups of small size and a decreasing number of groups or larger size.

(ii) The number of interconnections that exists among communities also follows a broad distribution, that provides some clues in the direction of the assessment of the *strength of weak ties theory*, foreseen by the early work of Granovetter [24].

(iii) The community structure of the network is defined, independently of the method adopted to unveil it. To this purpose, we take into account the possible bias introduced by the sampling procedures [36] and the resolution limit suffered by some types of community detection algorithms [37, 38].

(iv) The emergence of the so-called *small world phenomenon* - whose existence in real-world social networks has been assessed during the sixties by Milgram [23]: the community structure of the network is highly clustered and tightly interconnected by means of short paths, features which are exhibited by several small world networks [15, 39]. According to the model of *small world network* proposed by Watts and Strogatz [39], not only the diameter of the network grows as the logarithm of the size (a feature exhibited also by random networks), but also the clustering coefficient is high - a discriminating feature observed also in our case.

Methods

The aim of this work is to analyze the mesoscopic features of the community structure of the Facebook social network. In the following we provide some information about the process of data collection, briefly discussing the sampling methodology and the techniques adopted to collect data.

This is the first step to study the community structure of real-world networks, that reflect unique characteristics which are impossible to replicate by using synthetic network models [40].

After that, we discuss the process of community detection that we adopted to unveil the community structure of the network (and, to this regard, additional technical details are discussed in the Appendix).

Finally, we describe the process of definition of the community meta-network - a network whose nodes represent the communities identified in the social graph, to which it follows its analysis and discussion of findings.

Sampling the Facebook network

Differently from other online social network platforms (for example Twitter), Facebook does not provide a framework to automatically access information related to users with public profiles.

This lack of data availability has been faced acquiring public information directly from the platform, by means of a sampling process.

During this study we did not inspect, acquire or store personal information about users, since we were interested only in reconstructing the social connections among a sample of them - whose friend-lists were publicly accessible. To this purpose, we designed a Web data mining platform with the only ability to visit the publicly accessible friend-list Web pages of specific users, selected according to a sampling algorithm, and extract their connections. Obtained data have been used only to reconstruct the network sample studied in this work.

The architecture of the designed mining platform is briefly schematized as follows. We devised a data mining agent (*i.e.*, an autonomous software tool), which implements two sampling methodologies (*breadth-first search* and *uniform* sampling). The agent queries the Facebook server(s) in order to request the friend-list Web pages of specific users. In detail, the agent visits those Web pages containing the friend-list of a given user, following the directives of the chosen sampling methodology, and extracts the friendship relationships reported in the publicly accessible user profile.

The sampling procedure runs until any termination criterion/a is/are met (*e.g.*, a maximum running time, a minimum size of the sample, *etc.*), concluding the sampling process. Collected data are processed and stored in anonymized format,[a] post-processed, cleaned and filtered according to further requirements.

The sampling methodologies

In the following, we briefly discuss the two statistical sampling methods adopted in this work, namely the *breadth-first-search* and the *uniform* sampling.

The breadth-first-search sampling

The first adopted sampling methodology is a snowball technique that exploits the breadth-first-search (BFS), an uninformed graph traversal algorithm. Starting from a *seed node*, the procedure explores its neighborhood; then, for each neighbor, it visits its unexplored neighbors, and so on, until the whole network is visited (or, alternatively, a termination criterion is met). This sampling technique has several advantages with respect to other techniques (for example, *random walks* sampling, *forest fire* sampling, *etc.*) as discussed in recent literature [41, 42]. One of the main advantages is that it produces a coherent graph whose topological features can be studied.

For this reason it has been adopted in a variety of OSNs mining studies [1, 43–46]. During our experimentation, we defined the termination criterion that the mining process did not exceed 10 days of running time. By observing a short time-limit, we ensured a negligible effect of evolution of the network structure (less than 2% overall, according to a heuristic calculation based on the growth rate of Facebook during the sampling process - August 2010). The size of the obtained (partial) graph of the Facebook social network has been adopted as yardstick for the *uniform* sampling process.

The uniform sampling

The second chosen sampling methodology is a rejection-based sampling technique, called *uniform* sampling. The main advantage of this technique is that it is proven unbiased, at least in its formulation for Facebook. Details about its definition are provided by Gjoka *et al.* [44]. The process consists of generating an arbitrary number of user-IDs, randomly distributed in the domain of assignment of the Facebook user-ID system. In our case, it is the space of the 32-bit numbers: the maximum amount of assignable user-IDs is 2^{32}, about 4 billions. As of August 2010 (the period during which we carried out the sampling process), the number of subscribed users on Facebook was about 500 millions, thus the probability of randomly generating an existing user-ID was $\approx 1/8$.

The sampling process has been set up as follows: first we generated a number of random user-IDs, lying in the interval $[0, 2^{32} - 1]$, equal to the dimension of the BFS-sample multiplied by 8. Then, we queried Facebook for their existence. Our expectation was to obtain a sample of comparable dimensions with respect to the BFS-sample. Actually, we obtained a slightly smaller sample, due to the restrictive privacy settings imposed by some users, who configured their profile preventing the public accessibility of their friend-lists. The issue of the privacy has been investigated in our previous work [45].

Description of the samples

All the user-IDs contained in the samples have been anonymized using a 48-bit hashing functions [47], in order to hide references to users and their connections. Data have been post-processed for a cleansing step, during which all the duplicates have been removed, and their integrity and congruency have been verified. The characteristics of the samples are reported in Table 1. The size of both the samples is in the magnitude of few millions of nodes and edges.

The anonymized datasets studied in this work may be examined by the scientific community.[b]

Some of the statistical and topological features of these networks have been discussed in our previous work [45], and our main previous findings can be summarized as follows:

- It emerges that the degree distribution of nodes in the samples is defined by a power law $P(x) \propto x^{-\lambda}$ identifying two different regimes. In detail, it is possible to divide the domain into two intervals (tentatively $1 \leq x \leq 10$ and $x > 10$), whose exponents are $\lambda_1^{BFS} = 2.45$, $\lambda_2^{BFS} = 0.6$ and $\lambda_1^{UNI} = 2.91$, $\lambda_2^{UNI} = 0.2$ respectively for the BFS and the *uniform* sample, in agreement with recent studies by Facebook [18, 19].
- Concerning the diameter of the networks, the BFS sample shows a small diameter, in agreement with the *six-degrees of separation theory* [39], given the snowball nature of

Table 1 BFS and *uniform* samples description

Feature	BFS	Uniform
No. visited users	63.4K	48.1K
No. discovered neighbors	8.21M	7.69M
No. total edges	12.58M	7.84M
Size largest connected component	98.98%	94.96%
Avg. degree (visited users)	396.8	326.0
2nd largest eigenvalue	68.93	23.63
Effective diameter	8.69	14.72
Avg. clustering coefficient	$1.88 \cdot 10^{-2}$	$1.40 \cdot 10^{-3}$
Density	0.626%	0.678%

In this table we report some statistics regarding the two samples, BFS and *uniform*, which have been collected during August 2010 from the Facebook social network.

the sampling algorithm, which produces a plausible graph; differently, the diameter is over-represented in the *uniform* sample, possibly because the largest connected component does not cover the whole network.

- Regarding the *clustering coefficient*, we observed that the average values for both the samples are very high, similarly as reported by other recent studies on OSNs [3, 44]. High clustering coefficient and small diameter provide a clue of the presence of the so-called *small world* effect [15, 39] in the Facebook social graph.

Detecting communities

Given the large size of our Facebook samples, most of the community detection algorithms existing in literature could not deal with it. In order to unveil the community structure of these networks we adopted two computationally efficient techniques: (i) *Label Propagation Algorithm* (LPA) [48], and (ii) *Fast Network Community Algorithm* (FNCA) [49].

In the following we discuss the main advantages given from their choice and their performance.

Advantages and performance of chosen methods

The problem of selecting a particular community detection algorithm is crucial if the aim is to unveil the community structure of a network. In fact, the choice of a given methodology could affect the outcome of the experiments. In particular, several algorithms depend on tuning specific parameters, such as the size of the communities in the given networks, and/or their number (for additional information see recent surveys on this wide topic [30–35]).

In this study, the purpose was to unveil the unknown community structure of our Facebook samples, and to do so we choose two different techniques which rely just on the topology of the network itself as guide to discover the community structure.

LPA (Label Propagation Algorithm) is an algorithm for community detection based on the paradigm of label propagation, a common strategy characterizing several machine learning algorithms. Its computational cost is near liner with respect to the size of the analyzed network. This computational efficiency makes it well suited for the discovery of communities in large networks, such as in our case. LPA only exploits the network structure as guide and does not follow any pre-defined objective function to maximize (differently from FNCA); in addition, it does not require any prior information about the communities, their number or their size.

Table 2 Results on Facebook network samples

Algorithm	No. communities	Network modularity	Time (s)
BFS (8.21M vertices, 12.58M edges)			
FNCA	50,156	0.6867	$5.97 \cdot 10^4$
LPA	48,750	0.6963	$2.27 \cdot 10^4$
Uniform (7.69M vertices, 7.84M edges)			
FNCA	40,700	0.9650	$3.77 \cdot 10^4$
LPA	48,022	0.9749	$2.32 \cdot 10^4$

This table summarizes performance and results of the two chosen community detection algorithms (*i.e.*, FNCA and LPA) applied to the samples we collected from Facebook.

Table 3 Representation of a community structure

Community-ID	List of members
community-ID_1	{user-ID_a; user-ID_b; … ; user-ID_c}
community-ID_2	{user-ID_i; user-ID_j; … ; user-ID_k}
…	{…}
community-ID_N	{user-ID_x; user-ID_y; … ; user-ID_z}

To represent the community structure discovered in each sample we adopted the format reported in this table.

FNCA (Fast Network Community Algorithm) is a computationally efficient method to unveil the community structure of large networks. It is based on the maximization of an objective function called *network modularity* [50, 51]. Similarly to LPA, it does not require prior information on the structure of the network, the number of communities present in the network and/or their size.

Even though the paradigms on which the algorithms rely are different, a common feature emerges: their functioning is agnostic with respect to the characteristics of the considered network. This aspect makes them an ideal choice, considering that we do not have any prior information about the characteristics of the community structure of Facebook. Further technical details regarding these methods are discussed in the Appendix of this paper.

The performance of the LPA and FNCA on our Facebook samples is showed in Table 2. Both the algorithms are able to unveil the community structure of the network in double time. High values of *network modularity* have been obtained in both the samples. This aspect suggests the presence of a well-defined community structure.

The community structure has been represented by using a list of vectors which are identified by a 'community-ID'; each vector contains the list of user-IDs (in anonymized format) of the users belonging to the given community; an example is depicted in Table 3. This representation was instrumental to carry out with efficiency the experiments discussed in the remainder of the paper.

Assessing the quality of the community detection

Remarkably, one challenge arises in the context of the assessment of the quality of the community detection process in real-world scenarios that is the lack of a ground truth against which to compare the results provided by the adopted community detection strategy - which might be biased by the strategy itself [37, 38]. For such a reason, some works [52–54] estimate the quality of a community detection algorithm by measuring some internal measures of quality of detected communities, based on topological characteristics (for example, the network modularity to establish the density of connections among and within communities, or the stability of eigenvalues of the Laplacian graph). Other approaches [33] are based on the possibility of exploiting exogenous factors, such as semantic information derived from additional knowledge on users (for example their affiliations to particular groups, *etc.*). In the first case, indicators of internal quality of the communities are often not sufficient to ensure the quality of the results - think, for example, at the resolution limit that arises in modularity maximization algorithms [37, 38]. On the other hand, no additional information on users other than their interconnections was available to us, for the purpose of assessing the quality of our communities.

Then, to establish the significance of the community structure obtained by using the methods discussed above, we chose to evaluate the similarity of outcomes provided by the two adopted algorithms, against each other, in a number of different ways which are discussed in the next section. This might help in highlighting anomalies in our methodology, in case of significant divergences between obtained results.

Building the community meta-network

To study the mesoscopic features of the community structure of Facebook, we abstracted a *meta-network* consisting of the communities, as follows. We built a weighted undirected graph $G' = (V', E', \omega)$, whose set of nodes is represented by the communities constituting the given community structure. In G' there exists an edge $e'_{uv} \in E'$ connecting a pair of nodes $u, v \in V'$ if and only if there exists in the social network graph $G = (V, E)$ at least one edge $e_{ij} \in E$ which connects a pairs of nodes $i, j \in V$, such that $i \in u$ and $j \in v$ (*i.e.*, user i belongs to community u and user v belongs to community j). The weight function is defined as

$$\omega_{u,v} = \sum_{i \in u, j \in v} e_{ij} \tag{1}$$

(*i.e.*, the sum of the total number of edges connecting all users belonging to u and v).

Table 4 summarizes some characteristics of the networks obtained for the *uniform* sample by using FNCA and LPA. Something which immediately emerges is that the overall statistics obtained by using the two different community detection methods are very similar. The number of nodes in the *meta-networks* is smaller than the total number of communities discovered by the algorithms, because we excluded all those 'communities' containing only one member (whose consideration would be in antithesis with the definition of community in the common sense).

Table 4 Features of the meta-networks representing the *community structure* for the *uniform* sample

Feature	FNCA	LPA
No. nodes/edges	36,248/836,130	35,276/785,751
Min./Max./Avg. weight	1/16,088/1.47	1/7,712/1.47
Size largest conn. comp.	99.76%	99.75%
Avg. degree	46.13	44.54
2nd largest eigenvalue	171.54	23.63
Effective diameter	4.85	4.45
Avg. clustering coefficient	0.1236	0.1318
Density	0.127%	0.126%

In this table we report some statistics regarding the community structure *meta-network* obtained from the *uniform* sample, by using the two chosen community detection algorithms (*i.e.*, FNCA and LPA).

We discuss results regarding the community structure and its mesoscopic features in the following.

Results

The analysis of the community structure of Facebook will focus on the following aspects: (i) first, we try to evaluate the quality of the communities identified by means of the community detection algorithms described above. This step includes assessing the similarity of results obtained by using different sampling techniques and clustering methods. In detail, we evaluate the possible bias introduced by well-known limitations of these techniques (*e.g.*, the resolution limit for modularity maximization methods [37, 38] or the sampling bias due to the incompleteness of the sampling process [36]). (ii) Second, we investigate the mesoscopic features of the community *meta-network* considering some characteristics of the network (such as the diameter, the distribution of shortest-paths and weights of links, the connectivity among communities, *etc.*), discussing how these features may reflect organization patterns of individuals in the network.

Analysis of the community structure

In order to characterize the features of the community structure of Facebook, our first step was to describe the distribution of the size of the communities discovered. This feature has been investigated in current literature [12, 40], and it emerges that different complex networks exhibit heavy-tailed distributions in the size of the communities. This implies the existence of a large amount of communities whose size is very small and a very small amount of large communities in this type of real-world networks. In detail, Lancichinetti *et al.* [12] put into evidence that this holds true for a large family of complex networks, such as information, communication, biological, and social networks.

Distribution of the community size

Figures 1 and 2 represent the probability mass function of the distributions of the size of discovered communities, respectively for *uniform* and BFS sample, by using the two cho-

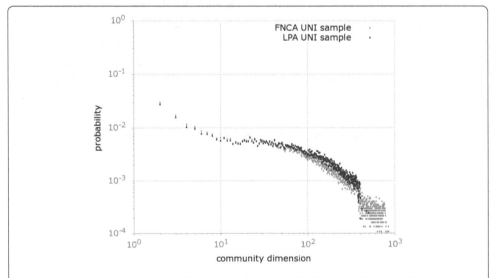

Figure 1 This plot shows the *probability mass function* of the distribution of the size of the communities discovered by the two adopted algorithms (*i.e.*, FNCA and LPA) for the *uniform* sample. Both the distributions are broad and heavy-tailed.

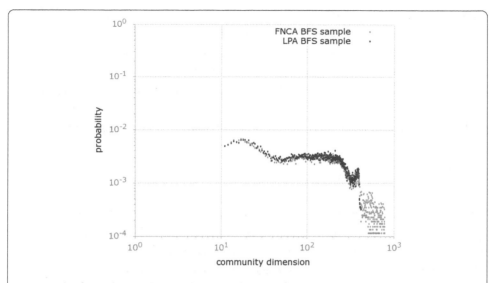

Figure 2 This figure depicts the *probability mass function* of the distribution of the size of the communities discovered by FNCA and LPA for the BFS sample. The distributions are wide but not heavy-tailed, due to the presence of a quasi-steady distribution of communities of size between 50 and 500.

sen community detection algorithms. From the analysis of these figures, it emerges that in both cases the distributions produced by the two community detection algorithms are very similar. Moreover, we can observe that these distributions are broad and resembles other real-world complex networks (*cf.* [12]).

From a further analysis it emerges that, for the *uniform* sample (Figure 1), both the distributions are broad and heavy-tailed. Differently, the distributions for the BFS sample are wide but not heavy-tailed, due to the quasi-steady probability of finding communities of size between 50 and 200.

The difference between BFS and *uniform* samples appears in agreement with the adopted sampling techniques. In fact, it has been recently put into evidence [36, 45] that a sampling algorithm such as the BFS may affect the degree distribution towards high degree nodes, in case of incomplete visits. Interestingly, this reflects also in the presence of communities, tentatively lying in the size interval $50 \geq x \geq 200$, that are in greater number with respect to what it would be expected by a scale-free network.

To the best of our knowledge, this is the first time it is observed that the bias towards high degree nodes introduced by the BFS sampling method reflects on the features of the community structure of a network. To the purpose of sampling, we could indicate as more appropriate those rejection-based methods, such as the *uniform* sampling, that do not over-represent high degree nodes.

Indeed, the analytical results reported in Table 2 combined with the plots discussed above, suggest that both the algorithms identified a similar amount of communities, regardless the adopted sampling method. This is also reflected by the similar values of *network modularity* obtained for the two different sets. Moreover, the size of the communities themselves seems to coincide for most of the times.

The following point we address is inspecting the quality of the community structure obtained by using FNCA and LPA. The possibility that two different algorithms produce different community structures is not to be excluded, thus in the following we investigate to what extent the results we obtained share a high degree of similarity.

Community structure similarity

In order to evaluate the similarity of two community structures we adopt three measures: (i) a variant of the *Jaccard coefficient*, called *binary Jaccard coefficient*; (ii) the *Kullback-Leibler divergence*; and, (iii) the *normalized mutual information*. In the following we discuss them separately, to explain their functioning, the motivations of their adoption and the obtained results.

The first measure considered to our purpose is the *binary Jaccard coefficient*, defined as

$$\hat{J}(\mathbf{v}, \mathbf{w}) = \frac{M_{11}}{M_{01} + M_{10} + M_{11}}, \tag{2}$$

where M_{11} represents the total number of shared elements between two vectors[c] $\mathbf{v}$ and $\mathbf{w}$, M_{01} represents the total number of elements belonging to $\mathbf{w}$ and not belonging to $\mathbf{v}$, and, finally M_{10} the *vice-versa*. The outcome of this measure lies in $[0, 1]$.

The adoption of the binary Jaccard coefficient is due to the following consideration: if we would compute the simple intersection of two sets (*i.e.*, the community structures) by using the classic Jaccard coefficient, those communities differing even by only one member would be considered different, while a high degree of similarity among them could still be envisaged. We avoid this issue adopting the binary Jaccard coefficient, by comparing each vector of the former set against all the vectors in the latter set, in order to *match* the most similar one. The mean degree of similarity is then computed as

$$\sum_{i=1}^{N} \frac{\max(\hat{J}(\mathbf{v}, \mathbf{w})_i)}{N}, \tag{3}$$

where $\max(\hat{J}(\mathbf{v}, \mathbf{w})_i)$ represents the highest value of similarity chosen among those calculated combining the vector i of the former set with all the vectors of the latter set. We obtained the results as in Table 5, in which we show the mean, median and standard deviations of the results obtained by comparing, both for the BFS and the *uniform* sample, the outcome of the clustering processes according to the two different algorithms (*i.e.*, FNCA and LPA).

While the number of identical communities between the two sets obtained by using, respectively, BFS and *uniform* sampling, is not high (*i.e.*, respectively, $\approx 2\%$ and $\approx 35\%$), the overall mean degree of similarity is very high (*i.e.*, $\approx 73\%$ and $\approx 91\%$). This is due to the high number of communities which differ only for a very small number of elements. Moreover, the fact that the median is, respectively, $\approx 75\%$ and $\approx 99\%$, and that the very majority of results lie in one standard deviation, supports the similarity of the obtained community structures.

Table 5 Similarity degree of community structures

Metric	Sample	Degree of similarity FNCA *vs.* LPA			
		Common	Mean	Median	Std. D.
$\hat{J}$	BFS	2.45%	73.28%	74.24%	18.76%
	uniform	35.57%	91.53%	98.63%	15.98%

In this table we report the results obtained computing the similarity between the community structure discovered by using FNCA and LPA in the BFS and *uniform* samples, computed by means of the binary Jaccard coefficient.

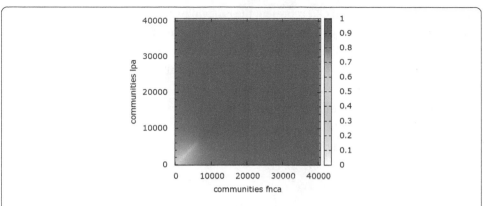

Figure 3 This heat-map highlights the similarity of the communities discovered by means of the two adopted algorithms (*i.e.*, FNCA and LPA) applied to the *uniform* sample. Almost the totality of communities discovered share a high fraction of members (in average the 91%), according the Jaccard similarity computed pairwisely selecting the most similar communities in the partitions.

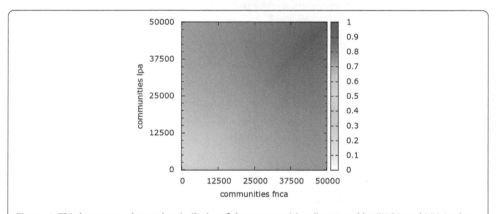

Figure 4 This heat-map shows the similarity of the communities discovered by FNCA and LPA in the **BFS sample.** In this case, with respect to the *uniform* sample case, the pairwise similarity between communities emerges slightly less obviously, but it is in average the 73%.

Figures 3 and 4 graphically highlight these findings. Their interpretation is as follows: on the *x-axis* and on the *y-axis* there are represented the communities discovered for the FNCA and the LPA methods, respectively. The higher the degree of similarity between two compared communities, the higher the heat-map scores. The similarity is graphically evident considering that the values of heat showed in the figures are very high (*i.e.*, greater than 0.7) for the most of the heat-map.

Before introducing the second experiment, observe that it is desirable to assess, not only if the two clustering solutions present a large amount of similar clusters, but also if they exhibit a similar statistical distribution in the size of the obtained clusters. To this purpose, a second method has been taken into consideration: the divergence measure called *Kullback-Leibler divergence*, that is defined as

$$D_{\mathrm{KL}}(P \parallel Q) = \sum_i P(i) \log \frac{P(i)}{Q(i)}, \tag{4}$$

where P and Q represent, respectively, the probability distributions that characterize the size of communities discovered by LPA and FNCA, calculated on a given sample. Let i be a given size such that $P(i)$ and $Q(i)$ represent the probability that a community of size i exists in the distributions P and Q. The KL divergence is helpful if one would like to calculate how different are two distributions with respect to one another. In particular, being the KL divergence defined in the interval $0 \leq D_{KL} \leq \infty$, the smaller the value of KL divergence between two distributions, the more similar they are.

We calculated the pairwise KL divergences between the distributions discussed above, finding the following results.

(i) on the *uniform* sample:

- $D_{KL}(P_{LPA} \parallel P_{FNCA}) = 7.722 \cdot 10^{-3}$
- $D_{KL}(P_{FNCA} \parallel P_{LPA}) = 7.542 \cdot 10^{-3}$

(ii) on the BFS sample:

- $D_{KL}(P_{LPA} \parallel P_{FNCA}) = 3.764 \cdot 10^{-3}$
- $D_{KL}(P_{FNCA} \parallel P_{LPA}) = 4.292 \cdot 10^{-3}$

The low values obtained by adopting the KL divergence put into evidence the correlation between the distributions calculated by using the two different algorithms on the two different samples.

Finally, to compute the quality of the results, we adopted a third measure, called *normalized mutual information* (NMI) [55]. Such a measure assumes that, given a graph G, a *ground truth* is available to verify what are the clusters (said *real clusters*) in G and what are their features. Let us denote as A the true community structure of G and suppose that G consists of c_A clusters. Let us consider a clustering algorithm applied on G and assume that it identifies a community structure B consisting of c_B clusters. We define a $c_A \times c_B$ matrix - said *confusion matrix* - CM such that each row of CM corresponds to a cluster in A whereas each column of CM is associated with a cluster in B. The generic element CM_{ij} is equal to the number of elements of the real ith cluster which are also present in the jth cluster found by the algorithm. Starting from these assumptions, the *normalized mutual information* is defined as

$$\text{NMI}(A, B) = \frac{-2 \sum_{i=1}^{c_A} \sum_{j=1}^{c_B} N_{ij} \log(\frac{N_{ij}N}{N_{i.}N_{.j}})}{\sum_{i=1}^{c_A} N_{i.} \log(\frac{N_{i.}}{N}) + \sum_{j=1}^{c_B} N_{.j} \log(\frac{N_{.j}}{N})} \tag{5}$$

being $N_{i.}$ (resp., $N_{.j}$) the sum of the elements in the ith row (resp., jth column) of the confusion matrix. If the considered clustering algorithm would work perfectly, then for each discovered cluster j, it would exist a real cluster i exactly coinciding with j. In such a case, it is possible to show that $\text{NMI}(A, B)$ is exactly equal to 1 [55]. By contrast, if the clusters detected by the algorithm are totally independent of the real communities then it is possible to show that the NMI is equal to 0. The NMI, therefore, ranges from 0 to 1 and the higher the value, the better the clustering algorithm performs with respect to the ground truth.

Observe that, in our scenario, we do not have at disposal any ground truth, given the fact that the community structure of the considered network is unknown and the purpose of our study was, in fact, to discover it. Still, we can adopt the NMI to compare against each other, the outcome of the clustering solutions obtained by means of two different algorithms, taking the result of the former and using it as a ground truth to assess the latter, or the *vice-versa*.

Several variants of *normalized mutual information* exist: to our purposes, we adopted two different versions of NMI, henceforth called NMI_{LFK} and NMI_{MGH} - after the authors initials - presented, respectively, by Lancichinetti, Fortunato and Kertesz [56] and by McDaid, Greene and Hurley [57]. These two variants adopt slightly different normalization factors, thus they produce different (but comparable) results.

Applying these two versions of NMI according to the considerations presented above, we obtained the following results:

(i) on the *uniform* sample:

- $NMI_{LFK}(FNCA_{uniform}, LPA_{uniform}) = 0.825$
- $NMI_{MGH}(FNCA_{uniform}, LPA_{uniform}) = 0.786$

(ii) on the BFS sample:

- $NMI_{LFK}(FNCA_{BFS}, LPA_{BFS}) = 0.678$
- $NMI_{MGH}(FNCA_{BFS}, LPA_{BFS}) = 0.648$

The high values obtained by using the *normalized mutual information*, which is able to better capture nuances and facets of different clustering solutions with respect to the much simpler binary Jaccard coefficient adopted above, still confirm the similarity of the community structure discovered by the two different algorithms employed in our analysis.

Given the limitations imposed by the lack of a ground truth for real-world networks for which the community structure is unknown, the approaches we adopted to assess the results are only a best-approximation of any robust evaluation method. Indeed, the problem of evaluating the clustering quality of real-world networks lacking of a ground truth is an open and urgent problem in current literature.

In addition, recently [37], in the context of detecting communities by adopting the *network modularity* as maximization function, a resolution limit has been put into evidence. In [37], the authors found that modularity optimization could, depending on the topology of the network, cause the inability of the process of community detection to find communities whose size is smaller than $\sqrt{E/2}$ (*i.e.*, in our case $\approx 3,000$). This reflects in another effect, that is the creation of big communities that include a large part of the nodes of the network, without affecting the global value of network modularity.

Being all the communities revealed smaller than that size and distributed in agreement with what already observed for other complex networks [12], we may hypothesize that the community structure unveiled by the algorithm for our samples is unlikely to be affected by the resolution limit.

Mesoscopic features of the community structure

In the following we consider the *uniform* sample and the community structure unveiled by the LPA as yardstick for our investigation. The experiments discussed in the remainder of this section focus in particular on three aspects: (i) assessment of the mesoscopic features of the community structure of the network and their implications in terms of social dynamics; (ii) study of the connectivity among communities and how it reflects on users organization patterns on a large scale; (iii) ability of inferring additional insights by means of visual observation of the community structure.

The purpose of investigating the mesoscopic features of the community structure of Facebook includes finding patterns that emerge from the network structure, in particular those which are related not to individuals or to the overall networks, but with those aggregation units that are the communities among which users gather.

To this purpose, we first discuss the degree distribution of communities discovered by means of our methods (*i.e.*, FNCA and LPA) in the *uniform* sample. We report Figure 5, that shows the complementary cumulative degree probability distribution (ccdf) as a function of the degree in the cases discussed above. The meaning of the *complementary cumulative distribution function (ccdf)*, defined as $F(x) = \Pr(X > x)$, is the probability that a random variable X assumes values below a given x. Analyzing these distributions we observe a very peculiar feature: two different regimes, tentatively $1 \le x < 100$ and $100 \le x < 300$, can be identified, and a cut-off in proximity of $x \approx 300$ as well. This reveals a decreasing chance of finding communities as their size grows, with a clear cut-off above a certain threshold. Interestingly, a similar phenomenon has been previously observed in the Facebook social graph [44] and it has been put in correlation with the so-called *self-organization* principle observed in social networks [58]. Self-organization is the ability of individual to coordinate and organize in patterns or structures which are proven to be efficient, robust and reliable. For example, efficiency could be expressed in terms of minimizing costs for diffusing information [59, 60], robustness could be represented by the presence of redundant connections that link the same groups and reliability by the ability of the network to well-react to errors and malfunctioning [61–63].

In the light of this observations, we tried to relate how communities grow with respect to their degree of connectivity. Our finding are reported in Figure 6. It emerges that, not only the communities above a certain threshold size are much less likely to happen, but also they are much less interconnected. In fact, we can observe that the average degree of communities grows proportionally to their size up to a cut-off value still approximately $x \approx$ 300. Above this threshold, larger communities become less and less connected with the others. This finding provides an argument in support to the idea that individuals in online social networks are mostly aggregated in small- or medium-size communities. On the other hand, large communities may suffer of a lack of external connectivity. The fact that

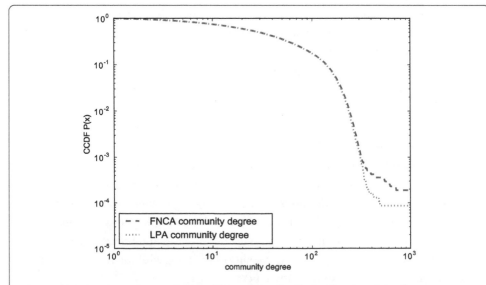

Figure 5 This plot shows the *complementary cumulative distribution function* of the degree distribution of the meta-network of communities discovered by the FNCA and LPA algorithms, for the *uniform* sample. In this kind of network, each node represents a community and each edge, whose weight is computed according to Equation (1), links communities whose members are connected in the original network. Results follow a heavy-tailed distribution and are very similar for both algorithms.

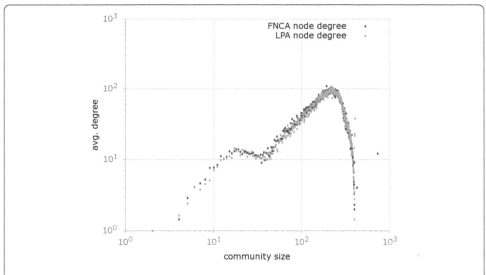

Figure 6 In this plot we show the average degree of communities expressed as a function of their size. It is possible to observe that the average degree grows proportionally to the size of the communities up to a certain threshold, approximately $x \approx 300$ above which the average degree of the communities quickly falls off.

individuals mostly aggregate in communities well-connected among each other without a coordinated effort is in line with the self-organization principle explained above.

Interestingly, self-organization is a phenomenon which is known to happen in *small world* networks [59, 60, 64, 65] and in their community structure [66]. In the light of this assumption, we investigated the presence of the *small world* effect in the community structure of Facebook. To this purpose, a reliable indicator of the presence of this phenomenon is the clustering coefficient - *i.e.*, the tendency to the creation of closed triangles among triads of communities. In our context, the clustering coefficient of a community is the ratio of the number of existing links over the number of possible links between the given community and its neighbors. Given our meta-network $G = (V, E)$, the clustering coefficient C_i of community $i \in V$ is

$$C_i = 2\left|\left\{(v,w)|(i,v),(i,w),(v,w) \in E\right\}\right|/k_i(k_i - 1),$$

where k_i is the degree of community i.

It can be intuitively interpreted as the probability that, given two randomly chosen communities that share a common neighbor, there also exists a link between them. High values of average clustering coefficient indicate that the communities are well connected among each other. This result would be interesting since it would indicate a tendency to the *small world* effect.

We plotted the average clustering coefficient probability distribution for the community structure in Figure 7. From its analysis it emerges that the slope of this curve is smooth, which allows for a the existence of a high probability of finding communities with large clustering coefficient, irrespectively of the number of connections they have with other communities.

This interesting fact reflects the existence of a tight and highly connected core in the community structure [25, 26]. The *small world* effect is also related to the presence of

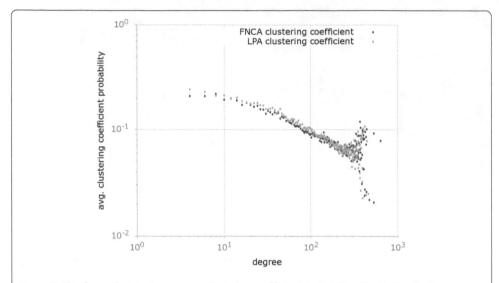

Figure 7 This figure depicts the average clustering coefficient probability distribution for the community meta-network computed according to FNCA and LPA in the *uniform* sample. Results provided by the two methods are comparable and the distribution of the average clustering coefficient as a function of the degree is broad.

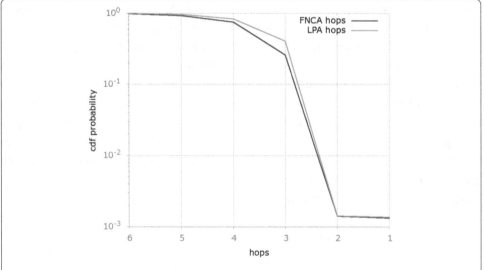

Figure 8 This plot shows the *cumulative distribution function* of the hops separating communities of the meta-network computed according to FNCA and LPA for the *uniform* sample. Almost the totality of communities are connected within 4 hops.

short-paths connecting communities. In this context, it is reasonable to suppose that, randomly selecting two disconnected communities, it is likely that a short path connecting their members exists.

To investigate this aspect, in the following we analyze the effective diameter and the shortest paths distribution in the community structure. To this purpose, Figure 8 reports the *cumulative distribution function* of the probability that two arbitrary communities are connected in a given number of hops. The *cumulative distribution function (cdf)* defines the probability that a random variable X assumes values below a given x. In that sense, from Figure 8 it emerges[d] that all communities are connected in a number of hops of 6, and most interestingly, that the highest advantage in terms of probability gain of connecting two randomly chosen communities, is obtained considering hops of length 3.

This aspect is further investigated as follows: Figure 9 represents the probability distribution for the shortest paths as a function of the path length. The interesting behavior which emerges from its analysis is that the shortest path probability distribution reaches a peak for paths of length 2 and 3. In correspondence with this peak, the number of connected pairs of communities quickly grows, reaching the effective diameter of the networks (*cf.* Figure 8). This findings has an important impact on the features of the overall social graph. In fact, if we would suppose that all nodes belonging to a given community are well connected each other, or even directly connected, this would result in a very short diameter of the social graph itself. In fact, there will always exist a very short path connecting the communities of any pair of randomly chosen members of the social network. Interestingly, this hypothesis is substantiated by recent studies by Facebook, who used heuristic techniques to measure the average diameter of the whole network [18, 19]. Their outcomes are very similar to our results: they estimated an average diameter of 4.72 while the effective diameter of the community structure for our *uniform* sample is 4.45 and 4.85, respectively for LPA and FNCA.

Thus, we conclude the characterization of the mesoscopic features of the community structure discussing the distribution of weights and strength of links among communities. The importance of this kind of analysis rises considering some social conjectures, like the Granovetter's *strength of weak ties theory* [24], that rely on the assessment of the strength of links in social networks. To this purpose, we resemble that the *strength* $s^{\omega}(v)$ (or *weighted degree*) of a given node v is determined as the sum of the weights of all edges incident on v, defined as

$$s^{\omega}(v) = \sum_{e \in I(v)} \omega(e),$$

where $\omega(e)$ is the weight of a given edge e and $I(v)$ the set of edges incident on v.

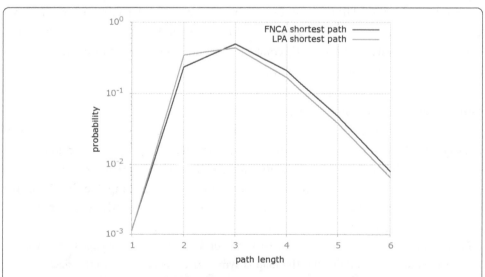

Figure 9 **This figure displays the shortest paths probability distribution for the meta-network of communities discovered by the FNCA and LPA algorithms in the *uniform* sample.** In agreement to Figure 8, the path length peak resides between 2 and 4.

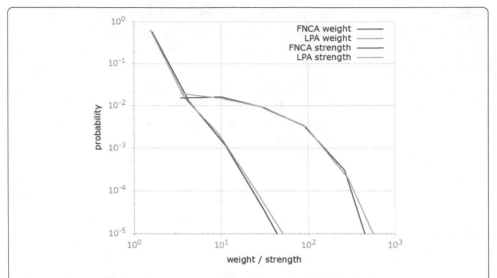

Figure 10 **This plot shows the probability distributions of weight and strength of edges of the meta-network of communities discovered by FNCA and LPA in the *uniform* sample.** The distribution of weights is scale-free and, regarding strength we can identify two different regimes.

In Figure 10, we plotted the probability distribution of both weight and strength on links among communities. Interestingly, the distribution of weights is defined by a power law $P(x) = x^{-\gamma}$ described by a coefficient $\gamma = 1.45$. The strength distribution is still broad but it is possible to observe two different regimes, in the intervals of tentatively $1 \leq x < 10^2$ and $x \geq 10^2$.

Given the definition of weights for the community meta-network, as in Equation (1) (*i.e.*, the sum of total number of edges connecting all users belonging to the two connected communities), we can suggest the hypothesis that there exists a high probability of finding a large number of pairs of communities whose members are not directly connected, and a increasingly smaller number of pairs of communities whose members are highly connected each other. These connections, which are usually referred as to *weak ties*, according to the *strength of weak ties theory* [24], are characterized by a smaller strength but a hightened tendency to proficiently connect communities otherwise disconnected. This aspect is further discussed in the following.

Connectivity among communities

The last experiment discussed in this paper is devoted to understanding the density of links connecting communities in Facebook. In particular, we are interested in defining to what extent links connect communities of comparable or different size. To do so, we considered each edge in the community *meta-network* and we computed the size of the community to which the *source node* of the edge belonged to. Similarly, we computed the size of the *target* community.[e]

Figure 11 represents a probability density map of the distribution of edges among communities. First, we highlight that the map is symmetric with respect to the diagonal, according to the fact that the graph is undirected and each edge is counted twice, once for each end-vertex. From the analysis of this figure, it emerges that edges mainly connect two types of communities: (i) communities of small size, each other - this is the most common

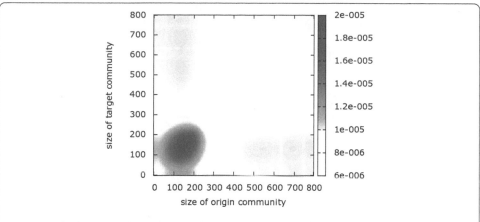

Figure 11 This heat-map shows the probability distribution map of links between communities of different size, computed by LPA in the *uniform* sample. It emerges the tendency of communities of smaller size to be strongly interconnected among each other.

case; (ii) communities of small size with communities of large size - less likely to happen but still significant.

This can be intuitively explained since the number of communities of small size is much greater than the number of large communities. On the other hand, it is an important finding since similar results have been recently described for Twitter [21], in the context of the evaluation of the Granovetter's *strength of weak ties theory* [24].[f]

In fact, according to this theory, weak links typically occur among communities that do not share a large amount of neighbors, and are important to keep the network proficiently connected.

Inter and intra-community links

For further analysis, we evaluated the amount of edges that fall in each given community with respect to its size. The results of this assessment are reported in Figure 12. The interpretation of this plot is the following: on the *y-axis* it is represented the fraction of edges per community as a function of the size of the community itself, reported on the *x-axis*. It emerges that also the distribution of the link fraction against the size of the communities follows a power law with an exponent equal to $x = 2.45$. This result shows that small communities are also more internally dense, while larger communities exhibit less internal connectivity - decreasing according to their size. Indeed, this result is different from that recently proved for Twitter [21], in which a Gaussian-like distribution has been discovered. This is probably due to the intrinsic characteristics of the networks, that are topologically dissimilar (*i.e.*, Twitter is represented by a directed graph with multiple type of edges) and also the interpretation itself of social tie is different. In fact, Twitter represents in a way *hierarchical connections* - in the form of *follower* and *followed* users - while Facebook tries to reflects a friendship social structure which better represents the community structure of real social networks.

The emergence of this scaling law is interesting with regard to the organization patterns that are reflected by individuals participating to large social networks. In fact, it seems that users that constitute small communities are generally very well connected to other communities and among each others, while large communities of individuals seem to be linked in a less efficient way to other communities - and also less dense of links. This is reflected

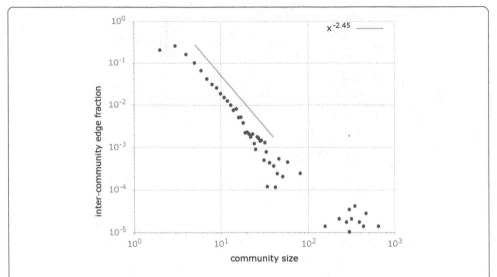

Figure 12 This figure depicts the probability distribution of the fraction of inter-community edges (*i.e.*, those edges that connects communities among each other) as a function of the size of the communities, according to the LPA community detection algorithm applied on the *uniform* sample. In agreement with Figure 11, a scale-free behavior emerges, highlighting that the majority of edges connects among each other communities of small size.

by the small number of weak ties incident on communities of large size with respect to the number of individuals they gather. These findings are relevant since they provide a clue that individuals are able to self-organize even in large networks and without a coordinated effort. This might improve their ability to efficiently get in touch and communicate with a number of users larger than their friends or acquaintances.

Visual observation of the community meta-network

The visual analysis of large-scale networks is usually unfeasible when managing samples whose size is in the order of millions of entities. Even though, by adopting our technique of building a community meta-network, it is yet possible to study the mesoscopic features of the Facebook social network from an unprecedented perspective. To this purpose, for example, social network analysts may be able to infer additional insights about the structure of the original network from the visual analysis of its community structure.

In Figure 13, obtained by using Cvis^g - a hierarchical-based circular visualization algorithm - we represent the community structure unveiled by LPA in the *uniform* sample. From its analysis, it is possible to appreciate the existence of a tight core of communities which occupy a central position into the meta-network [25, 26]. A further inspection of the features of these communities revealed that their positioning is generally irrespective of their size. This means that there are several different small communities which play a dominant role in the network. This is in agreement with previous findings and highlight the role of self-organization on such a scale. Similar considerations hold for the periphery of the network, which is constituted both by small and larger communities.

Finally, we highlight the presence of so-called *weak ties*, that proficiently connect communities that otherwise would be far each other. In particular, those that connect communities in the core with communities in the periphery of the network, according to the *strength of weak ties theory* [24], might represent the most important patterns along which

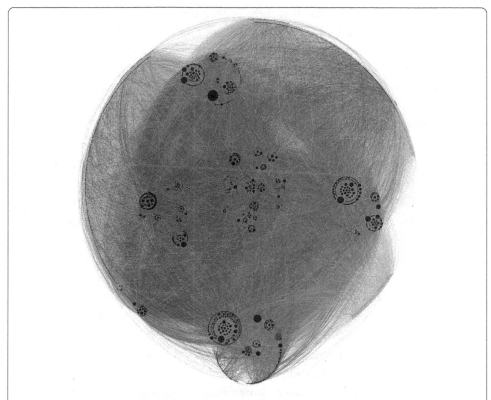

Figure 13 This figure displays the outcome of a hierarchical-based circular visualization algorithm that represents the community structure unveiled by LPA in the *uniform* sample. It emerges the existence of a tight core of communities which occupy a central position into the meta-network, generally irrespectively of their size.

communications flow, enhancing users ability of getting in touch with each other, efficiently spreading information, and so on.

Discussion

This work concludes putting into evidence implications, strength and limitations of our study.

First of all, in this paper we put into evidence that the community structure of the Facebook social network presents a broad distribution of the dimension of the communities, similarly to other complex networks [12]. This result is independent with respect to the algorithm adopted to discover the community structure, and even (but in a less evident way) to the sampling methodology adopted to collect the samples. On the other hand, this is the first experimental work that proves the hypothesis, theoretically advanced by [36], of the possible bias towards high degree nodes introduced by the BFS sampling methodology for incomplete sampling of large networks.

Regarding the qualitative analysis of our results, it emerges that the communities share a high degree of similarity among different samples.

The analysis of the community meta-network puts into evidence different mesoscopic features. We discovered that the average degree of communities average degree of communities and their size put into evidence the tendency to self-organization of users into small- or medium-size communities well-connected among each other.

Our further analysis highlights that there exists a tendency to the creation of short-paths (whose length mainly consists of two or three hops), that proficiently connect the majority of the communities existing in the network. This finally led us to the identification of links connecting communities otherwise disconnected, that we called *weak ties* in the Granovetter's sense [24].

Results in context with previous literature

Several recent studies focused on the analysis of the community structure of different social networks [12, 13, 40, 67]. An in-depth analysis of the Facebook collegiate networks has been carried out in [13]. Authors considered data collected from 5 American colleges and examined how the online social lives reflect the real social structure. They proved that the analysis of the community structure of online social networks is fundamental to obtain additional insights about the prominent motivations which underlie the community creation in the corresponding real world. Moreover, authors found that the Facebook social network shows a very tight community structure, and exhibits high values of network modularity. Some of their findings are confirmed in this study on a large scale.

Recently [12], it has been put into evidence that the community structure of social networks shares similarities with communication and biological networks. The authors investigated several mesoscopic features of different networks, such as community size distribution, density of communities and the average shortest path length, finding that these features are very characteristic of the network nature. According to their findings, we assessed that also Facebook is well-described by some specific characteristics on a mesoscopic level.

Regarding the mesoscale structure analysis of social networks, [40] provided a study by comparing three state-of-the-art methods to detect the community structure on large networks. An interesting aspect considered in that work is that two of the three considered methods can detect overlapping communities, so that a differential analysis has been carried out by the authors. They focused on the analysis of several mesoscopic features such as the community size and density distribution and the neighborhood overlapping. In addition, they verified that results obtained by the analysis of synthetic networks are profoundly different from those obtained by analyzing real-world datasets, in particular regarding the community structure, putting into evidence the emergence of need of studying online social networks acquiring data from the real platforms. Their findings are also confirmed in this study, in which we acquired a sample of the social graph directly from the Facebook platform.

An interesting work which is closely related to this study regards the assessment of the *strength of weak ties theory* in the context of Twitter [21]. In that work, it emerges that one of the roles of weak ties is to connect small communities of acquaintances which are not that close to belong to the same community but, on the other hand, are somehow proficiently in contact. Clues in this direction come also from this study, although the two networks exhibit different topological features (*i.e.*, Twitter is represented by a directed graph with multiple type of edges) and also carry a different interpretation of the social connections themselves. In fact, social ties in Twitter represent *hierarchical connections* (in the form of *follower* and *followed* users), while Facebook tries to reflects a friendship social structure which better represents the community structure of real-world social networks.

Concluding, recently [67] the perspective of the study of the community structure has been *revisited* considering the problem of the detecting communities of edges instead of the classical communities of nodes. In this approach we observe an interesting feature, *i.e.*, that link communities intrinsically incorporate the concept of overlap. The authors findings are applied to large social networks of mobile phone calls confirming the emergence of scale free distributions also for link community structures. Similar studies could be extended to online social networks like Facebook, in order to investigating the existence of particular communication patterns or motifs.

Strength and limitations of this study

In the following we discuss the main strengths and limitations of this study. To the best of our knowledge, this is the first work that investigates the general mesoscopic structure of a large online social network. This is particularly interesting since it is opposed to just trying to identify dense clusters in large communities, which is the aim of different works discussed above.

This work highlights the possibility of inferring characteristics describing the organization patterns of users of large social networks, analyzing some mesoscopic features that arise from a statistical and topological investigation. This kind of analysis has been recently carried out for some types of social media platforms (such as Twitter [21]) which capture different nuances of relations (for example, hierarchical follower-followed user relations), but there was a lack in literature regarding online social network platforms reflecting friendship relations, such as Facebook. This work, that tries to fill this gap, provides results that well relate with those presented in recent literature, and describes novel insights on the problem of characterizing social network structure on the large scale.

We can already envision two limitations of this work, which leave space for further investigation. First, our sample purely relies on binary friendship relations, which represent the simplest way to capture the concept of friendship on Facebook. On the other hand, there could be more refined representations of the Facebook social graph, such as taking into consideration the frequency of interaction among individuals of the network, to weight the importance of each tie. To this purpose, the feasibility of this study is complicated by the privacy issues deriving from accessing private information about users habits (such as the frequency of interaction with their friends), which limit our range of study.

Depending on this aspect, the second shortcoming of this study rises. In detail, the fact that we were concerned with the analysis of publicly accessible profiles implies that our sample only reproduces a partial picture of the Facebook social network which could slightly vary with respect to the overall social graph. To this purpose, another aspect which deserves more investigation is understanding how the incompleteness of the sampling affects the characteristics of the community structure.

Conclusions

The aim of this work was to investigate the emergence of social dynamics, organization patterns and mesoscopic features in the community structure of a large online social network such as Facebook. This task was quite thrilling and not trivial, since a number of theoretical and computational challenges raised.

First of all, we collected real-world data directly from the online network. In fact, as recently put into evidence in literature [40], the differences between synthetic and real-world data have profound implications on results.

After we reconstructed a sample of the structure of the social graph of Facebook, we unveiled its community structure. The main findings that emerged from the mesoscopic analysis of the community structure of this network can be summarized as follows:

(i) We assessed the tendency of online social network users to constitute communities of small size, proving the presence of a decreasing number of communities of larger size. This behavior explains the tendency of users to self-organization even in absence of a coordinated effort.

(ii) We investigated the occurrence of connections among communities, finding that some kind of links, commonly referred as to *weak ties*, are more relevant than others because they connect communities each other, according to the Granovetter's *strength of weak ties theory* [24] and in agreement with recent studies on other online social networks such as Twitter [21].

(iii) The community structure is highly clusterized and the diameter of the community structure meta-network is small (approximately around 4 and 5). These aspects indicate the presence of the *small world phenomenon*, which characterizes real-world social networks, according to sociological studies envisioned by Milgram [23] and in agreement with some heuristic evaluations recently provided by Facebook [18, 19].

The achieved results open space for further studies in different directions. As far as it concerns our long-term future research directions, we plan to investigate, amongst others, the following issues:

(i) Devising a model to identify the most representative users inside each given community. This would leave space for further interesting applications, such as the maximization of advertising on online social networks, the analysis of communication dynamics, spread of influence and information and so on.

(ii) Exploiting geographical data regarding the physical location of users of Facebook, to study the effect of strong and weak ties in the society [24]. In fact, is it known that a relevant additional source of information is represented by the geographical distribution of individuals [68–70]. For example, we suppose that strong ties could reflect relations characterized by physical closeness, while weak ties could be more appropriate to represent connections among physically distant individuals.

(iii) Concluding, we devised a strategy to estimate the strength of ties between social network users [71] and we want to study its application to online social networks on a large scale. In the case of social ties, this is equivalent to estimate the friendship degree between a pair of users by considering their interactions and their attitude to exchange information.

Appendix

In this appendix we shortly discuss the background in community detection algorithms and explain the functioning of the two community detection methods adopted during our experimentation, namely LPA and FNCA.

Community detection in complex networks

The problem of discovering the community structure of a network has been approached in several different ways. A common formulation of this problem is to find a partitioning $V = (V_1 \cup V_2 \cup \cdots \cup V_n)$ of disjoint subsets of vertices of the graph $G = (V, E)$ representing the network (in which the vertices represent the users of the network and the edges represent their social ties) in a meaningful manner.

The most popular quantitative measure to prove the existence of an emergent community structure in a network, called *network modularity*, has been proposed by Girvan and Newman [50, 51]. It is defined as the sum of the difference between the fraction of edges falling in each given community and the expected fraction if they were randomly distributed. Let consider a network which has been partitioned into m communities; its value of network modularity is

$$Q = \sum_{s=1}^{m} \left[\frac{l_s}{|E|} - \left(\frac{d_s}{2|E|} \right)^2 \right] \tag{6}$$

assuming l_s the number of edges between vertices belonging to the sth community and d_s the sum of the degrees of the vertices in the sth community. High values of Q imply high values of l_s for each discovered community. In that case, detected communities are dense within their structure and weakly coupled among each other.

Partitioning a network in disjoint subsets may arise some difficulties. In fact, each user in the network possibly belongs to several different communities; the problem of overlapping community detection has recently received a lot of attention (see [34]). Moreover, may exist networks in which a certain individual may not belong to any group, remaining isolated, as recently put into evidence by Hunter *et al.* [16]. Such a case commonly happens in real and online social networks, as reported by recent social studies [72].

Community detection techniques

In its general formulation, the problem of finding communities in a network is solvable assigning each vertex of the network to a cluster, in a meaningful way. There exist different paradigms to solve this problem, such as the spectral clustering [73, 74] which relies on optimizing the process of cutting the graph, and the *network modularity* maximization methods.

Regarding spectral clustering techniques, they have an important limitation. They require a prior knowledge on the network, to define the number of communities present in the network and their size. This makes them unsuitable if the aim is to unveil the unknown community structure of a given network.

As for network modularity maximization techniques, the task of maximizing the objective function Q has been proved NP-hard [75], thus several heuristic techniques have been presented during the last years. The Girvan-Newman algorithm [50, 51, 76] is an example. It exploits the assumption that it is possible to maximize the value of Q deleting edges with a high value of betweenness, starting from the intuition that they connect vertices belonging to different communities. Unfortunately, the cost of this algorithm is $O(n^3)$, being n the number of vertices in the network; it is unsuitable for large-scale networks. A tremendous amount of improved versions of this approach have been provided in the last years and are extensively discussed in [30, 31].

From a computational perspective, some of the state-of-the-art algorithms are *Louvain method* [77, 78], LPA [48, 79], FNCA [49] and a voltage-based divisive method [80]. All these algorithms provide with near linear computational costs.

Recently, the problem of discovering the community structure in a network including the possibility of finding overlapping nodes belonging to different communities at the same time, has acquired a lot of attention by the scientists because of the seminal paper presented by Palla *et al.* [81]. A lot of efforts have been spent in order to advance novel possible strategies. For example, an interesting approach has been proposed by Gregory [82], that is based on an extension of the Label Propagation Algorithm adopted in this work. On the other hand, an approach in which the hierarchical clustering is instrumental to find the overlapping community structure has been proposed by Lancichinetti *et al.* [56, 83].

Label Propagation Algorithm (LPA)

The LPA (Label Propagation Algorithm) [48] is a near linear time algorithm for community detection. Its functioning is very simple, considered its computational efficiency. LPA uses only the network structure as its guide, is optimized for large-scale networks, does not follow any pre-defined objective function and does not require any prior information about the communities. Labels represent unique identifiers, assigned to each vertex of the network.

Its functioning is reported as described in [48]:

Step 1 To initialize, each vertex is given a unique label;

Step 2 Repeatedly, each vertex updates its label with the one used by the greatest number of neighbors. If more than one label is used by the same maximum number of neighbors, one is chosen randomly. After several iterations, the same label tends to become associated with all the members of a community;

Step 3 Vertices labeled alike are added to one community.

Authors themselves proved that this process, under specific conditions, could not converge. In order to avoid deadlocks and to guarantee an efficient network clustering, we accept their suggestion to adopt an *asynchronous* update of the labels, considering the values of some neighbors at the previous iteration and some at the current one. This precaution ensures the convergence of the process, usually in few steps. Raghavan *et al.* [48] ensure that five iterations are sufficient to correctly classify 95% of vertices of the network. After some experimentation, we found that this forecast is too optimistic, thus we elevated the maximum number of iterations to 50, finding a good compromise between quality of results and amount of time required for computation.

A characteristic of this approach is that it produces groups that are not necessarily contiguous, thus it could exist a path connecting a pair of vertices in a group passing through vertices belonging to different groups. Although in our case this condition would be acceptable, we adopted the suggestion of the authors to devise a final step to split the groups into one or more contiguous communities.

The authors proved its near linear computational cost [48].

Fast Network Community Algorithm (FNCA)

FNCA (Fast Network Community Algorithm) [49] is a modularity maximization algorithm for community detection, optimized for large-scale social networks.

Given an unweighted and undirected network $G = (V, E)$, suppose the vertices are divided into communities such that vertex i belongs to community $r(i)$ denoted by $c_r(i)$; the function Q is defined as Equation (7), where $A = (A_{ij})_{n \times n}$ is the adjacency matrix of network G. $A_{ij} = 1$ if node i and node j connect each other, $A_{ij} = 0$ otherwise. The δ function $\delta(u, v)$ is equal to 1 if $u = v$ and 0 otherwise. The degree k_i of any vertex i is defined to be

$k_i = \sum_j A_{ij}$ and $m = \frac{1}{2}\sum_{ij} A_{ij}$ is the number of edges in the network

$$Q = \frac{1}{2m}\sum_{ij}\left(\left(A_{ij} - \frac{k_i k_j}{2m}\right) \times \delta\big(r(i), r(j)\big)\right). \tag{7}$$

We convert Equation (7) to Equation (8), which takes the function Q as the sum of functions f of all nodes. The function f can be regarded as the difference between the number of edges that fall within communities and the expected number of edges that fall within communities, from the local angle of any node in the network. The function f of each node can measure whether a network division indicates a strong community structure from its local point of view

$$Q = \frac{1}{2m}\sum_i f_i, \quad f_i = \sum_{j \in c_{r(i)}}\left(A_{ij} - \frac{k_i k_j}{2m}\right). \tag{8}$$

The authors [49] proved that: (i) any node in a network can evaluate its function f only by using local information (the information of its community); (ii) if the variety of some nodes label results in the increase of its function f and the labels of the other nodes do not change, the function Q of the whole network will increase too. The community detection algorithm used is based on these assumptions. It makes each node maximize its own function f by using local information in the sight of local view, which will then achieve the goal that optimize the function Q.

Moreover, in complex networks with a community structure, holds true the intuition that any node should have the same label with one of its neighbors or it is itself a cluster. Therefore, each node does not need to compute its function f for all the labels at each iteration, but just for the labels of its neighbors. This improvement not only decreases the time complexity of the algorithm, but also makes it able to optimize the function Q by using only local information of the network community structure.

It has been proved that this algorithm, under certain conditions, could not quickly converge, thus we introduced an iteration number limitation T as additional termination condition. Experimental results show that, the clustering solution of FNCA is good enough before 50 iterations for most large-scale networks. Therefore, iteration number limitation T is set at 50 in all the experiments in this paper. Authors proved the near linear cost of this algorithm [49].

Competing interests
The author declares that he has no competing interests.

Author's contributions
EF designed and performed research, prepared figures, carried out empirical analysis, wrote and reviewed the manuscript.

Acknowledgements
The author is grateful to A. Flammini, B. Gonçalves, A. Lancichinetti, F. Menczer, F. Radicchi, and J.J. Ramasco for comments and suggestions on the manuscript.

Endnotes
[a] Data are represented in a compact format in order to save I/O operations and then are anonymized, in order not to store any kind of private data (such as the user-IDs).
[b] http://www.emilio.ferrara.name/datasets/.
[c] Remind that the vectors taken into account represent the communities of the network.
[d] To this regard, we put into evidence that the *x-axis* is reversed and we recall that the diameter of the considered community structures is 4.45 and 4.85, respectively for LPA and FNCA.

[e]   We recall that, being the network model adopted undirected, the meaning of source and target node is only instrumental to identify the end-vertex of each given edge.

[f]   The roles of weak ties is to connect small communities of acquaintances which are not that close to belong to the same community but, on the other hand, are somehow proficiently in contact.

[g]   https://sites.google.com/site/andrealancichinetti/cvis.

References

1. Mislove A, Marcon M, Gummadi K, Druschel P, Bhattacharjee B (2007) Measurement and analysis of online social networks. In: Proceedings of the 7th ACM SIGCOMM conference on internet measurement, pp 29-42
2. Zinoviev D, Duong V, Foley A, Voithofer R, Erhabor E, Mann R, Gwadry-Sridhar F, Bowman S, Soer J, Hasna A et al (2009) Toward understanding friendship in online social networks. Int J Technol Knowl Soc 5(2):1-8
3. Wilson C, Boe B, Sala A, Puttaswamy K, Zhao B (2009) User interactions in social networks and their implications. In: Proceedings of the 4th ACM European conference on computer systems. ACM, New York, pp 205-218
4. Ferrara E, Fiumara G, Baumgartner R (2010) Web data extraction, applications and techniques: a survey. Technical report
5. Heer J, Shneiderman B (2012) Interactive dynamics for visual analysis. ACM Queue 10(2):1-30
6. Boccaletti S, Latora V, Moreno Y, Chavez M, Hwang D (2006) Complex networks: structure and dynamics. Phys Rep 424(4-5):175-308
7. Backstrom L, Huttenlocher D, Kleinberg J, Lan X (2006) Group formation in large social networks: membership, growth, and evolution. In: Proceedings of the 12th ACM SIGKDD international conference on knowledge discovery and data mining. ACM, New York, pp 44-54
8. Leskovec J, Lang K, Dasgupta A, Mahoney M (2008) Statistical properties of community structure in large social and information networks. In: Proceeding of the 17th international conference on World Wide Web. ACM, New York, pp 695-704
9. Lozano S, Arenas A, Sánchez A (2008) Mesoscopic structure conditions the emergence of cooperation on social networks. PLoS ONE 3(4):e1892
10. Karrer B, Levina E, Newman M (2008) Robustness of community structure in networks. Phys Rev E 77(4):046119
11. Leskovec J, Lang K, Dasgupta A, Mahoney M (2009) Community structure in large networks: natural cluster sizes and the absence of large well-defined clusters. Internet Math 6:29-123
12. Lancichinetti A, Kivelä M, Saramäki J (2010) Characterizing the community structure of complex networks. PLoS ONE 5(8):e11976
13. Traud A, Kelsic E, Mucha P, Porter M (2011) Comparing community structure to characteristics in online collegiate social networks. SIAM Rev 53:526-546
14. Nishikawa T, Motter A (2011) Discovering network structure beyond communities. Sci Rep 1:151
15. Kleinberg J (2000) The small-world phenomenon: an algorithm perspective. In: Proceedings of the thirty-second annual ACM symposium on theory of computing. ACM, New York, pp 163-170
16. Hunter D, Goodreau S, Handcock M (2008) Goodness of fit of social network models. J Am Stat Assoc 103(481):248-258
17. Centola D (2010) The spread of behavior in an online social network experiment. Science 329(5996):1194-1197
18. Backstrom L, Boldi P, Rosa M, Ugander J, Vigna S (2011) Four degrees of separation. Arxiv preprint. arXiv:1111.4570
19. Ugander J, Karrer B, Backstrom L, Marlow C (2011) The anatomy of the facebook social graph. Arxiv preprint. arXiv:1111.4503
20. Ratkiewicz J, Fortunato S, Flammini A, Menczer F, Vespignani A (2010) Characterizing and modeling the dynamics of online popularity. Phys Rev Lett 105(15):158701
21. Grabowicz P, Ramasco J, Moro E, Pujol J, Eguiluz V (2012) Social features of online networks: the strength of intermediary ties in online social media. PLoS ONE 7:e29358
22. Conover M, Gonçalves B, Flammini A, Menczer F (2012) Partisan asymmetries in online political activity. EPJ Data Sci 1:6
23. Milgram S (1967) The small world problem. Psychol Today 2:60-67
24. Granovetter M (1973) The strength of weak ties. Am J Sociol 78:1360-1380
25. Borgatti S, Everett M (1999) Models of core/periphery structures. Soc Netw 21:375-395
26. Everett M, Borgatti S (1999) Peripheries of cohesive subsets. Soc Netw 21:397-407
27. Goldenberg J, Libai B, Muller E (2001) Using complex systems analysis to advance marketing theory development: modeling heterogeneity effects on new product growth through stochastic cellular automata. AMS Review 9(3):1-18
28. Goldenberg J, Libai B, Muller E (2001) Talk of the network: a complex systems look at the underlying process of word-of-mouth. Mark Lett 12(3):211-223
29. Zhou X, Xu Y, Li Y, Josang A, Cox C (2012) The state-of-the-art in personalized recommender systems for social networking. Artif Intell Rev 37(2):119-132
30. Porter M, Onnela J, Mucha P (2009) Communities in networks. Not Am Math Soc 56(9):1082-1097
31. Fortunato S (2010) Community detection in graphs. Phys Rep 486(3-5):75-174
32. Coscia M, Giannotti F, Pedreschi D (2011) A classification for community discovery methods in complex networks. Stat Anal Data Min 4(5):512-546
33. Tang L, Wang X, Liu H (2011) Community detection via heterogeneous interaction analysis. Data Min Knowl Discov 25(1):1-33
34. Xie J, Kelley S, Szymanski B (2011) Overlapping community detection in networks: the state of the art and comparative study. Arxiv preprint. arXiv:1110.5813
35. Newman M (2011) Communities, modules and large-scale structure in networks. Nat Phys 8:25-31
36. Kurant M, Markopoulou A, Thiran P (2010) On the bias of BFS (Breadth First Search). In: Proceedings of the 22nd international teletraffic congress. IEEE Press, New York, pp 1-8

37. Fortunato S, Barthélemy M (2007) Resolution limit in community detection. Proc Natl Acad Sci USA 104:36
38. Good B, de Montjoye Y, Clauset A (2010) Performance of modularity maximization in practical contexts. Phys Rev E 81(4):046106
39. Watts D, Strogatz S (1998) Collective dynamics of 'small-world' networks. Nature 393(6684):440-442
40. Tibély G, Kovanen L, Karsai M, Kaski K, Kertész J, Saramäki J (2011) Communities and beyond: mesoscopic analysis of a large social network with complementary methods. Phys Rev E 83(5):056125
41. Leskovec J, Faloutsos C (2006) Sampling from large graphs. In: Proceedings of the 12th ACM SIGKDD international conference on knowledge discovery and data mining. ACM, New York, pp 631-636
42. Kurant M, Markopoulou A, Thiran P (2011) Towards unbiased BFS sampling. IEEE J Sel Areas Commun 29(9):1799-1809
43. Chau D, Pandit S, Wang S, Faloutsos C (2007) Parallel crawling for online social networks. In: Proceedings of the 16th international conference on World Wide Web. ACM, New York, pp 1283-1284
44. Gjoka M, Kurant M, Butts C, Markopoulou A (2010) Walking in Facebook: a case study of unbiased sampling of OSNs. In: Proceedings of the 29th conference on information communications. IEEE Press, New York, pp 2498-2506
45. Catanese S, De Meo P, Ferrara E, Fiumara G, Provetti A (2011) Crawling Facebook for social network analysis purposes. In: Proceedings of the international conference on web intelligence, mining and semantics, pp 52:1-52:8
46. Ferrara E (2012) Community structure discovery in Facebook. Int J Soc Netw Min 1:67-90
47. Partow A General purpose hash function algorithms. http://www.partow.net/programming/hashfunctions/
48. Raghavan U, Albert R, Kumara S (2007) Near linear time algorithm to detect community structures in large-scale networks. Phys Rev E 76(3):036106
49. Jin D, Liu D, Yang B, Liu J (2009) Fast complex network clustering algorithm using agents. In: Proceedings of the 8th international conference on dependable, autonomic and secure computing, pp 615-619
50. Girvan M, Newman M (2002) Community structure in social and biological networks. Proc Natl Acad Sci USA 99(12):7821
51. Newman M, Girvan M (2004) Finding and evaluating community structure in networks. Phys Rev E 69(2):026113
52. Hu Y, Ding Y, Fan Y Di Z (2010) How to measure significance of community structure in complex networks. Arxiv preprint. arXiv:1002.2007v1
53. Yang Y, Sun Y, Pandit S, Chawla N, Han J (2011) Is objective function the silver bullet? A case study of community detection algorithms on social networks. In: 2011 international conference on advances in social networks analysis and mining. IEEE Press, New York, pp 394-397
54. Yang J, Leskovec J (2012) Defining and evaluating network communities based on ground-truth. Arxiv preprint. arXiv:1205.6233v1
55. Danon L, Díaz-Guilera A, Duch J, Arenas A (2005) Comparing community structure identification. J Stat Mech Theory Exp 2005:P09008
56. Lancichinetti A, Fortunato S, Kertész J (2009) Detecting the overlapping and hierarchical community structure in complex networks. New J Phys 11:033015
57. McDaid AF, Greene D, Hurley N (2011) Normalized mutual information to evaluate overlapping community finding algorithms. http://arxiv.org/abs/1110.2515
58. Anderson P (1999) Complexity theory and organization science. Organ Sci 10(3):216-232
59. Rosvall M, Sneppen K (2006) Modeling self-organization of communication and topology in social networks. Phys Rev E 74:016108
60. Latora V, Marchiori M (2001) Efficient behavior of small-world networks. Phys Rev Lett 87(19):198701
61. Albert R, Jeong H, Barabási A (2000) Error and attack tolerance of complex networks. Nature 406(6794):378-382
62. Dodds P, Watts D, Sabel C (2003) Information exchange and the robustness of organizational networks. Proc Natl Acad Sci USA 100(21):12516
63. Crucitti P, Latora V, Marchiori M (2004) Model for cascading failures in complex networks. Phys Rev E 69(4):045104
64. Barabási A, Albert R (1999) Emergence of scaling in random networks. Science 286(5439):509-512
65. Barrat A, Barthelemy M, Pastor-Satorras R, Vespignani A (2004) The architecture of complex weighted networks. Proc Natl Acad Sci USA 101(11):3747
66. Arenas A, Danon L, Diaz-Guilera A, Gleiser P, Guimera R (2004) Community analysis in social networks. Eur Phys J B, Condens Matter Complex Syst 38(2):373-380
67. Ahn Y, Bagrow J, Lehmann S (2010) Link communities reveal multiscale complexity in networks. Nature 466(7307):761-764
68. Onnela J, Saramäki J, Hyvönen J, Szabó G, Lazer D, Kaski K, Kertész J, Barabási A (2007) Structure and tie strengths in mobile communication networks. Proc Natl Acad Sci USA 104(18):7332
69. Wang D, Pedreschi D, Song C, Giannotti F, Barabási A (2011) Human mobility, social ties, and link prediction. In: 17th ACM SIGKDD conference on knowledge discovery and data mining (KDD 2011)
70. Onnela J, Arbesman S, González M, Barabási A, Christakis N (2011) Geographic constraints on social network groups. PLoS ONE 6(4):e16939
71. De Meo P, Ferrara E, Fiumara G, Ricciardello A (2012) A novel measure of edge centrality in social networks. Knowl-Based Syst 30:136-150
72. Hampton K, Sessions L, Her E, Rainie L (2009) Social isolation and new technology. Pew Internet & American Life Project, Washington, DC
73. Ng A, Jordan M, Weiss Y (2001) On spectral clustering: analysis and an algorithm. In: Advances in neural information processing systems 14: proceeding of the 2001 conference, pp 849-856
74. Hagen L, Kahng A (2002) New spectral methods for ratio cut partitioning and clustering. IEEE Trans Comput-Aided Des Integr Circuits Syst 11(9):1074-1085
75. Brandes U, Delling D, Gaertler M, Gorke R, Hoefer M, Nikoloski Z, Wagner D (2008) On modularity clustering. IEEE Trans Knowl Data Eng 20(2):172-188
76. Newman M (2006) Modularity and community structure in networks. Proc Natl Acad Sci USA 103(23):8577
77. Blondel V, Guillaume J, Lambiotte R, Lefebvre E (2008) Fast unfolding of communities in large networks. J Stat Mech Theory Exp 2008:P10008
78. De Meo P, Ferrara E, Fiumara G, Provetti A (2011) Generalized Louvain method for community detection in large networks. In: Proceedings of the 11th international conference on intelligent systems design and applications

79. Leung I, Hui P, Lio P, Crowcroft J (2009) Towards real-time community detection in large networks. Phys Rev E 79(6):066107
80. Wu F, Huberman B (2004) Finding communities in linear time: a physics approach. Eur Phys J B, Condens Matter Complex Syst 38(2):331-338
81. Palla G, Derényi I, Farkas I, Vicsek T (2005) Uncovering the overlapping community structure of complex networks in nature and society. Nature 435(7043):814-818
82. Gregory S (2007) An algorithm to find overlapping community structure in networks. In: Knowledge discovery in databases: PKDD 2007, pp 91-102
83. Lancichinetti A, Radicchi F, Ramasco J (2011) Finding statistically significant communities in networks. PLoS ONE 6(4):e18961

2

Exploiting citation networks for large-scale author name disambiguation

Christian Schulz[1], Amin Mazloumian[1], Alexander M Petersen[2], Orion Penner[2] and Dirk Helbing[1]*

*Correspondence:
dhelbing@ethz.ch
[1] Department of Humanities and
Social Sciences, Chair of Sociology,
in particular of Modeling and
Simulation, ETH Zurich,
Clausiusstrasse 50, CH-8092 Zurich,
Switzerland
Full list of author information is
available at the end of the article

Abstract

We present a novel algorithm and validation method for disambiguating author names in very large bibliographic data sets and apply it to the full Web of Science (WoS) citation index. Our algorithm relies only upon the author and citation graphs available for the whole period covered by the WoS. A pair-wise publication similarity metric, which is based on common co-authors, self-citations, shared references and citations, is established to perform a two-step agglomerative clustering that first connects individual papers and then merges similar clusters. This parameterized model is optimized using an *h*-index based recall measure, favoring the correct assignment of well-cited publications, and a name-initials-based precision using WoS metadata and cross-referenced Google Scholar profiles. Despite the use of limited metadata, we reach a recall of 87% and a precision of 88% with a preference for researchers with high *h*-index values. 47 million articles of WoS can be disambiguated on a single machine in less than a day. We develop an *h*-index distribution model, confirming that the prediction is in excellent agreement with the empirical data, and yielding insight into the utility of the *h*-index in real academic ranking scenarios.

Keywords: name disambiguation; citation analysis; clustering; *h*-index; science of science

1 Introduction

The ambiguity of author names is a major barrier to the analysis of large scientific publication databases on the level of individual researchers [1, 2]. Within such databases researchers generally appear only as they appear on any given publication i.e. by their surname and first name initials. Frequently, however, hundreds or even thousands of individual researchers happen to share the same surname and first name initials. Author name disambiguation is therefore an important prerequisite for the author level analyses of publication data. While many important and interesting problems can be examined without individual level data [3, 4] a great many other require such data to get to the real heart of the matter. Good examples include the role of gender in academic career success [5], whether ideas diffuse through the popularity of individual publications or the reputation of the authors [6, 7], how the specific competencies and experience of the individual authors recombine to search the space of potential innovations [8, 9], and whether one can predict scientific carriers [10–14]. Indeed, the importance of getting individual level data has been widely acknowledged, as can be seen in recent large scale initiatives to create disambiguated researcher databases [15, 16].

Algorithmic author name disambiguation is challenging for two reasons. First, existing disambiguation algorithms have to rely on metadata beyond author names to distinguish between authors with the same name, much like some administrative institutions do when they distinguish citizens with the same name based on attributes such as date and place of birth. However, in existing large-scale publication databases – such as Thomson Reuter's Web of Science (WoS) – metadata is often sparse, especially for older publications. Second, disambiguation algorithms may draw false conclusions when faced with incomplete metadata. For instance, when researchers change disciplines they transition to an entirely different part of the citation graph. Therefore, disambiguation algorithms that heavily rely on journal metadata to reconstruct researchers' career trajectories can easily represent such researchers with two different researcher profiles. This issue can be present in any case where an individual metadata (disciplinary profile, collaborators, affiliation) is not consistent over time.

Existing disambiguation algorithms typically exploit metadata like first and middle names, co-authors, publication titles, topic keywords, journal names, and affiliations or email addresses (for an overview see [2]). Reference [17] (and enhanced in [18]) presents a comprehensive method that includes all metadata of the MEDLINE database. The use of citation graph data is less common however, since only a few databases include this information. Previous examples to exploit such data include [19] which mainly relies on self-citations, and [20] that used shared references, but only for the disambiguation of two author names. Both retrieve data from the WoS, which is also used in [21] and [22], however, without exploiting the citation graph. Reference [21] had access to a manually maintained database of Italian researchers as a gold standard, while [22] found a ground truth in Dutch full professor publication lists.

Here, we develop and apply a novel author disambiguation algorithm with the explicit goal of measuring the h-index of researchers using the entire WoS citation index database. Introduced by Hirsch in 2005, the h-index is the most widely used measure of an individual's scientific impact. An individual's h-index is equal to the number h of publications that are cited at least h times. It is increasingly used in both informal and formal evaluation and career advancement programs [23]. However, despite its rapidly increasing popularity and use, very little is known about the overall distribution of h-indices in science. While an h-index of 30 is certainly less frequent than an h-index of 20, it is unknown how much less frequent. Models have been developed to estimate the distribution based upon some simple assumptions, but at best, they relied on incomplete data. Perhaps the most straightforward starting point for considering the distribution of h-index would be Lotka's law scientific for productivity [24], however in the results section we will show that the empirical data deviates significantly from a Pareto power-law distribution.

The most complete data-centric work to date is that of [25], who calculated a probability distribution $P(h)$ of h-indices using over 30,000 career profiles acquired via Google Scholar. Indeed this work represents a critical step forward in terms of understanding the overall distribution of h-indices and the high level dynamics that shape it. However, Google Scholar profiles are biased towards currently active and highly active researchers. As a consequence, their approach may underestimate the number of individuals with low h-index. A proper understanding of the entire h-index distribution $P(h)$ is critical to shaping policies and best practices of using it for scientific performance. Furthermore, as research becomes more interdisciplinary, the variation of h-index distribution across disciplines must be better understood to prevent biased evaluations. To tackle these and similar challenges, we present an algorithm that is optimized towards reproducing the correct h-index of researchers, makes use of the citation network, and is applicable for the entire dataset of WoS.

This manuscript will be laid out in the following manner. First, we will describe our algorithm, novel validation & optimization approach, and implementation details. Then we will present the results of our optimization procedure and the empirical h-index distribution produced by our algorithm. We will compare the empirical distribution to the predictions of a simple theoretical h-index model, which together show excellent agreement.

2 Methodology

2.1 The disambiguation algorithm

As discussed above, the goal of a disambiguation algorithm is to generate sets of publications that can be attributed to specific, individual, researchers. Our algorithm accomplishes this by a two step agglomerative approach (see Figure 1).

In the first step the goal is to determine if two papers were likely coauthored by the same individual. To that aim, we are using a similarity score approach to cluster papers. We first calculate the pairwise similarity between all pairs of papers in the dataset of ambiguous names. The similarity score (s_{ij}) between two papers i and j is calculated as follows:

$$s_{ij} = \alpha_A \left(\frac{|A_i \cap A_j|}{\min(|A_i|, |A_j|)} \right) + \alpha_S \left(|p_i \cap R_j| + |p_j \cap R_i| \right)$$
$$+ \alpha_R \left(|R_i \cap R_j| \right) + \alpha_C \left(\frac{|C_i \cap C_j|}{\min(|C_i|, |C_j|)} \right). \tag{1}$$

For each paper p_i we denote the reference list as R_i; the co-author list as A_i; the set of citing papers as C_i. Hence in this instantiation of the algorithm, these are the only three pieces of information one must have available for each paper. The $\cap$-operator together with the enclosing $|\ |$-operator count the number of common attributes. The first term in Eq. (1) measures the number of co-authors shared by two papers. The second term detects potential self-citations, a well recognized indicator of an increased probability of authorship by the same individual [26]. The third term is the count of common references between the two papers. The fourth term represents the number of papers that cite both publications. The first and last terms are normalized by a technique known as overlap coefficient [27]. It accounts for the higher likelihood of finding similarities when both co-author lists are very long or both publications are well-cited.

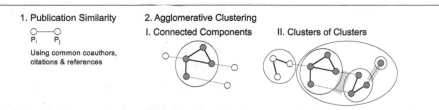

Figure 1 For a given set of publications, a measure for publication similarity is used to identify clusters that ideally represent unique researchers. First, the clustering creates strongly connected components. Second, well-linked clusters are merged.

Once all pairwise similarities have been calculated, our algorithm moves on to the first of two clustering processes (see Figure 1). In this first clustering we start by establishing a link between each pair of papers (i, j), for which the similarity score s_{ij} is greater than a threshold β_1. Then, each connected component (set of papers that can be reached from each other paper by traversing the previously created links) is labeled as a cluster. The goal is, of course, that all papers in any given cluster belong to one specific author.

In the second clustering process a new similarity score is calculated between all clusters generated in the previous step. Labeling one cluster by γ and another by κ the similarity between the clusters is calculated as follows:

$$S_{\gamma,\kappa} = \sum_{i \in \gamma j \in \kappa} \frac{s_{ij} \Theta(s_{ij} > \beta_2)}{|\gamma||\kappa|}. \tag{2}$$

Here $|\gamma|$ is the number of publications in cluster γ, similarly for $|\kappa|$. For this step we calculate the similarity between publications in separate clusters. The overall cluster-cluster similarity is the sum of the s_{ij} similarity weights that are above a certain threshold β_2, normalized by the number of papers of the two clusters. A link is then established between the two clusters if the new cluster similarity score ($S_{\gamma,\kappa}$) is greater than a threshold β_3. Each connected component (set of clusters that can be reached from each other cluster by traversing links) is then merged into a single cluster. Remaining individual papers are added to a cluster if they have a similarity score s_{ij} above a threshold β_4 with any paper in that cluster. We denote the set of clusters $\{K_i\}$ finally resulting from our algorithm. Each cluster is a set of papers and should ideally contain all papers published by one specific researcher.

2.2 Optimization and validation

The output of such an algorithm must be validated thoroughly by establishing error rates, specifying their dependence on the size of the researcher profiles produced. Here we develop two techniques for estimating the rates of the two types of statistical errors: (i) Type I errors ("splitting"), which split an individual's publications across two or more clusters, and (ii) Type II errors ("lumping"), which fail to distinguish between two or more author publication sets, i.e. an author mistakenly gets assigned papers from another author. Parameter optimization is a key step in arriving at a functional algorithm (see Figure 2). Our optimization approach differs from many other algorithms in that our optimization procedure does not only seek to minimize "lumping" and "splitting", but also to optimize an additional specified dimension defined by the research question one wishes to investigate with the disambiguated data. For this work, the dimension of interest is reproducing the h-index of individual researchers with high accuracy. Below we describe the details of our algorithm, and then we explain the optimization and validation procedures that we have developed with a specific focus on how to reach the h-index accuracy objective.

To assess lumping errors we start by extracting from the WoS database all papers in which a given surname appears in the author field. We then apply our algorithm to this set, ignoring the initials or first names associated with each instance of the given surname. This differs from the typical starting point of previous disambiguation efforts, where the underlying algorithms would be applied to the set of papers in which a given surname together with specific first initial. However, by omitting the first initial information we

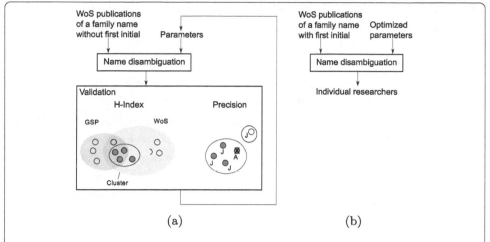

Figure 2 Optimization and validation procedure. (a) Parameters of the name disambiguation algorithm (shown in Figure 1) are optimized using Google Scholar Profiles (GSP) for measuring recall and first name initials for measuring precision. **(b)** For disambiguating the whole Web of Science (WoS), family names complemented by first initials.

determine an upper bound for the lumping error, as measured by precision. We define precision of a cluster i which contains various first name initials indexed by j:

$$P_i = \frac{\max_j(Frequency[FirstNameInitial(j, K_i)])}{|K_i|}. \tag{3}$$

Take the surname "Smith", for example. Applying the algorithm to all papers with that surname we get a set of clusters. We can assume that in each cluster the initial that appears on most papers is the "correct" initial, and all other initials are likely errors. For example in the cluster where "J" is the most frequent initial for "Smith" the precision can be estimated as the number of papers with the initial "J" divided by the overall number of papers in the cluster. Not all papers with "J" may correspond to the same person ("Jason" versus "John"), but in the absence of an absolute gold standard this serves as a proxy.

To assess the rate of splitting errors we draw upon Google Scholar Profile (GSP) data. Within an individual's Google Scholar Profile all of an author's publications (indexed by Google Scholar) can be found and we use these profiles as a gold standard. Currently, we have acquired GS profiles for 3,000 surnames. As one would expect, some errors exists within these profiles and papers can be mis-assigned. However, as we discuss below by optimizing for the reconstruction of the h-index, this is not a big concern. Before a GSP can be used as a gold standard the contents of the profile must first be cross-referenced to the WoS database by measuring distances in year, title, author list and journal information. A publication is cross-referenced if there is sufficient similarity in multiple fields and if there is no other publication that would also qualify as a match. Once a gold standard publication list has been arrived at, it is straightforward to use it to calculate our algorithm's recall for that profile:

$$R_\alpha = \frac{\max(|K_i \cap \mathrm{GSProfile}_\alpha|)}{|\mathrm{GSProfile}_\alpha \cap \mathrm{WoS}|}. \tag{4}$$

This is the recall value for a specific GSP (researcher α). It corresponds to the percentage of papers in the given profile (that we managed to cross-reference to WoS) that are also in the algorithm-generated cluster which contains most papers of that profile.

The recall value is a measure of how completely we have captured an individual's publication list. However, this does not, necessarily, indicate how well we have captured the portion of an individual's publication list that is relevant to our objective of accurately reproducing the h-index. Specifically, when the goal is to measure the h-index it is more important to assign every paper that contributes to an individual's h-index (the most cited) to his or her cluster, rather than to assign every single paper correctly. Of course, this amplifies the importance of correctly assigning highly cited papers. To measure the extent to which our algorithm can reproduce the h-index, we introduce a measure of the h-index recall:

$$R_\alpha^h = \frac{h(\max(|K_i \cap \text{GSProfile}_\alpha|))}{h(|\text{GSProfile}_\alpha \cap \text{WoS}|)}. \tag{5}$$

With the objective of producing the highest quality h-index estimates, this measure seamlessly replaces the typical recall measure as a way to evaluate the completeness of clusters. Thus we use it for our optimization and validation procedure instead of Eq. (4). However, it is necessary we make clear that in using this h-index centric measure the resulting disambiguation is optimized with regards to reproducing h-index distribution, but may not be optimal with regards to other criteria. Indeed if a reader were to apply our algorithm, or one like it, with a different goal in mind we advise them to adapt the recall measure to their specific goal.

2.3 Implementation

With about 47 million papers (for the analyzed period from 1900 to 2011), 141 million co-author entries, and 526 million citations referring to other articles within the database, the WoS is one of the largest available metadata collections of scientific articles and thus needs to be processed efficiently. While we concentrated on a few features (co-authors and citation graph), our framework can be extended to further metadata as well. We also do not make use of the full citation and co-author network when evaluating a single paper, in the sense that we do not traverse the graph to another paper node which is not directly connected to the paper in question. As a pre-processing step, we compute all publication similarity terms without applying concrete disambiguation parameters. For the complete WoS, we created 4.75 billion links between pairs of papers that have significant similarity and a common name (surname plus first initial). Publication similarity has a computational complexity of $O(n^2)$, where n is the number of papers of the ambiguous name. To reduce the cost of a single paper pair comparison, all information related to a single name is loaded into memory, whereas all feature data (mainly integer IDs) are stored in sorted arrays. For papers that have a publication year difference greater than 5, the computation is skipped to decrease the number of comparisons. This process took 11 hours on standard laptop hardware. Disambiguating the 5.6 million author names, i.e. weighting the similarity links and performing the two-step clustering took less than an hour. For the validation, we kept data for the 500 name networks in memory (consuming less than 4 GB) to test multiple parameter configurations subsequently, so that each parameter test (disambiguation and validation of the 500 names) could be executed in about 5 seconds.

3 Results

3.1 Optimizing disambiguation parameters

For the seven model parameters (α_A, α_S, α_R, α_C, β_2, β_3, β_4, while β_1 is fixed to 1), we want to find a configuration that minimizes both mean h-index error and mean precision error:

$$R^h_{\text{error}} = \langle 1 - R^h \rangle, \qquad P_{\text{error}} = \langle (1 - P)\sqrt{|K|} \rangle. \tag{6}$$

This mean P_{error} can be artificially small because it is averaged over (mostly) small clusters which easily achieve high precision. Hence, in the definition of our optimization scheme we introduce a counterbalancing statistical weight that accounts for size by requiring the algorithm to preferentially optimize the large clusters due to the cost incurred if any large cluster's precision error value, $1 - P$, is high. Relying on basic statistical arguments, the natural weight that we should give the large clusters is the statistical fluctuation scale attributable to size, which is proportional to square root of the size of the cluster. This weight also compensates for the fact that there are more smaller clusters than large clusters. In practice, this means that for two clusters of different sizes $K_+ = fK_-$ (with $f > 1$), then the larger cluster with K_+ will need to have a precision error equal to $(1 - P_-)/\sqrt{f}$ in order to contribute the same to the overall P_{error} value which must be minimized by the algorithm.

Due to the simplicity of our algorithm, we can conduct an extensive sampling over the whole parameter space. The results in Figure 3(a) show that there is a clear trade-off between the two types of errors and a lower limit that can be reached by our implementation. Our test data consists of 3,000 surnames that were randomly selected from WoS and where at least one profile could be found on Google Scholar. To further improve the result, we did an iterative local search on a 7-dimensional sphere around the best previous parameter configurations, starting with the best results from the random parameter sampling. For efficiency reasons and for cross-validation, we drew four random subsets with 500 surnames each and optimized them individually. In Figure 3(a), we aim at an error

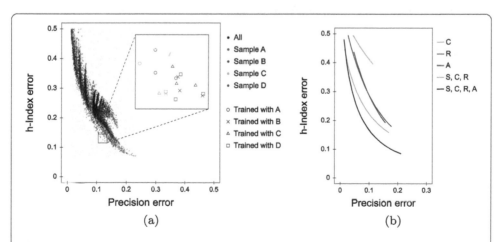

(a)   (b)

Figure 3 Optimizing disambiguation parameters. (a) 10,000 random disambiguation parameters were tested for the 3,000 family names which we can validate with Google Scholar profiles. Results (indicated as black dots) close to the origin $(0, 0)$ yield the best trade-off between precision and h-index correctness. For samples A, B, C and D (consisting of 500 family names each), parameters were further optimized independently and cross-validated. **(b)** Curves represent a lower hull estimate for the results of a random parameter sampling when using only certain features of the metadata (C – Citations, R – References, A – Authors, S – Self-citations). The closer the curves come to the origin, the smaller the error. The combination of all four features lead to the best h-index reconstruction.

that equally prefers a high h-index and precision correctness. We find

$$\alpha_A = 0.54, \qquad \alpha_S = 0.75, \qquad \alpha_R = 0.19, \qquad \alpha_C = 1.02,$$

$$\beta_2 = 0.19, \qquad \beta_3 = 0.011, \qquad \beta_4 = 0.49$$

which leads to a precision error of 11.84% and an h-index error of 12.63%. Co-authorship α_A comes out as a strong indicator for disambiguation, although co-author names are not disambiguated beforehand and hence represent a potential source of errors. Self-citations α_S are also highly weighted, but a self-citation link alone is not sufficient to exceed the threshold $\beta_1 = 1$ to form clusters.

Figure 3(b) shows how much the individual features (terms of Eq. (1)) contribute to the optimal solution. We fitted curves to the best results of a random sampling for a varying error trade-off, when only certain features are used (i.e. parameter of the other features are set to 0). Individual features cannot reach low error rates on their own. Combining features of the co-author and citation graph work best. Including more features like affiliations, topical features extracted from titles, summaries or keyword lists could potentially further improve the solution.

Size dependent biases can skew aggregate algorithm performance measures especially when there is a broad underlying heterogeneity in the data. Hence, stating mean error rates is not sufficient to fully understand the strengths and weaknesses of a disambiguation algorithm. In Figure 4(a) we show that our algorithm works better for larger profiles, i.e. researchers that have a higher h-index, which is not a surprising result since there is much more co-author and citation graph information than for people with only a few papers. On the other hand, precision is slowly decreasing for more common names, see Figure 4(b), which becomes an issue when disambiguating very large databases, where certain combinations of surname plus first initial can result in initially undisambiguated clusters comprising around ten thousand publications.

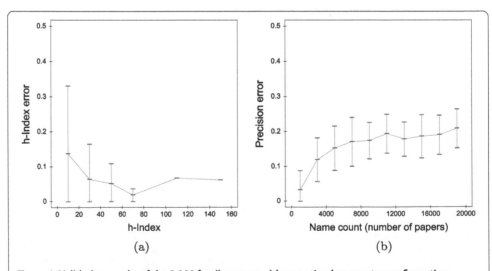

(a)   (b)

Figure 4 Validation results of the 3,000 family names with an optimal parameter configuration.
(a) The mean h-index error (bin width = 20, error bars displaying standard deviation) is decreasing for clusters with higher h-index. **(b)** The precision error is increasing with more common names (bin width = 2,000).

3.2 Further validation

We further evaluated the performance of our disambiguation method with four additional tests using different data or techniques. While each measures recall or precision, these performance indicators have different definitions and deviate here from our previous validation, but fit better with measures typically reported in past disambiguation work.

We performed a manual disambiguation validation similar to the one in [18]. 100 publication pairs were randomly chosen from all pairs of publications that our algorithm co-clustered. Another 100 random pairs were selected from the set in which each pair belongs to the same name, but were placed in different clusters. Students were asked to determine for an author name and a given pair of publications, if they were written by the same author or different authors. When uncertain, the student could choose "Not sure". Although all resources could be used, this is often a challenging task and especially voting for "Different authors" frequently required evidence beyond that was easily available. From 138 answers, we obtained 111 "Same authors", of which 94 were in the same clusters (a recall of about 84.7%), and 27 times "Different authors", of which all were correctly disambiguated to different clusters (a precision of 100%). We point out that a manual disambiguation may be biased towards easy cases that could receive a confident answer, however, it does provide further evidence of the suitability of our algorithm.

Another test for precision can be constructed from second initials metadata which we do not consider for our disambiguation algorithm (only first initials when clustering the whole WoS). Indeed, about 4.7 million clusters contain at least two second initial names. Here, for each cluster the most common second initial forms the set of correctly disambiguated publications (names that omit the second initial were ignored). We measure a mean precision of about 95.4%.

As a third way to evaluate precision, we "artificially" generated ground truth data by merging the sets of publications with two random names and then cluster them. The idea is that while we cannot say something about the correctness of the resulting clusters for one name, we can definitely show that the clustering is wrong when a cluster is generated from publications from both names. About 3,000 name pairs led to 26,887 clusters of which 18 clusters contained both names.

Our final additional validation is an estimate of recall, again for the whole disambiguated WoS. We evaluated about 870,000 arXiv.org publications, their metadata and fulltexts. From the PDFs more than half of all publications contained one or more email addresses. An email address is assumed to be a good indicator that, when two publications also share an author name, that this refers to the same unique researcher. Both arXiv and WoS provide DOIs for newer publications (starting around the year 2000), so cross-referencing was not an issue. We generated 110,011 "email" clusters, i.e. sets of publications that we also wanted to see for our disambiguation being put in one cluster. The mean recall was 98.1%.

3.3 Empirical h-index distribution and theoretical model

Using the optimized parameters, we disambiguated the complete WoS database containing about 5.6 million author names that have a unique surname plus first initial. While the true h-index distribution is not exactly known, we can compare it to the subset of rare names – names for which we assume require little if any disambiguation. We define rare names as surnames where for the whole WoS there is only one type of initial and that initial is itself very rare (q, x, z, u, y, o, and w), which results in 87,000 author names. The disambiguation of the rare names tells us that they indeed represent to a large extent unique researchers. Unfortunately, for higher h-index values $h > 20$ (values in the top 3% when excluding clusters with $h = 0,1$) the rare surnames are underrepresented with respect to the whole database (see Figure 5 for the comparison between the rare dataset and the full dataset h-index distributions). However, this difference is consistent with deviations arising from finite-size effects, since the rare dataset is significantly smaller than the entire dataset.

The empirical distribution $P(h)$ is a mixture of h-indices of scientists with varying discipline citation rates and varying longevity within mixed age-cohort groups. Hence, it may at first be difficult to interpret the mean value $\langle h \rangle$ as a representative measure for a typical scientist, since a typical scientist should be conditioned on career age and disciplinary factors. Nevertheless, in this section we develop a simple mixing model that predicts the expected frequencies of h, hence providing insight into several underlying features of the empirical "productivity" distribution $P(h)$.

Our h-index distribution model is based on the following basic assumptions:

1. The number of individuals of "career age" t in the aggregate data sample is given by an exponential distribution $P_1(t) = \exp[-t/\lambda_1]/\lambda_1$. We note that in this large-scale analysis we have not controlled for censoring bias since a large number of the careers analyzed are not complete, and so the empirical data likely overrepresent the number of careers with relatively small t.

2. The h-index growth factor $g_i \approx \langle h_i(t+1) - h_i(t) \rangle$ is the characteristic annual change in h_i of a given scientist, and is distributed according to an exponential distribution $P_2(g) = \exp[-g/\lambda_2]/\lambda_2$. The quantity g captures unaccounted factors such as the author-specific citation rate (due to research quality, reputation, and other various career factors), as well as the variation in citation and publication rates across discipline. For sake of simplicity, we assume that g_i is uncorrelated with t_i.

Hence, the index $h_i = g_i t_i$ of an individual i is simply given by the product of a career age t_i and growth factor g_i. The aggregate h-index distribution model $P_m(h)$ is derived from the distribution of a product of two random variables, t and g, each distributed exponentially by $P_1(t; \lambda_1)$ and $P_2(g; \lambda_2)$, respectively. Since both $g \geq 0$ and $t > 0$, the distribution $P(h)$ is readily calculated by

$$P_m(h) = \int_0^\infty \frac{dx}{x} P_1(x) P_2(h/x) = \frac{2}{\lambda_1 \lambda_2} K_0 \left(2\sqrt{h/(\lambda_1 \lambda_2)} \right),$$

where $K_0(x)$ is the Modified Bessel function of the second kind. The probability density function $P_m(h)$ has mean $\langle h \rangle = \lambda_1 \lambda_2$, standard deviation $\sqrt{3}\langle h \rangle$, and asymptotic behavior $P_m(h) \sim \exp[-\sqrt{h/\langle h \rangle}]/h^{1/4}$ for $h \gg 1$.

Figure 5(a) shows the empirical distribution $P(h)$ for 4 datasets, analyzing only clusters with $h \geq 2$ in order to focus on clusters that have at least two cited papers which satisfy our similarity threshold with at least one other paper. Surprisingly, each $P(h)$ is well fit by the theoretical model $P_m(h; \lambda_1 \lambda_2)$ with varying $\lambda_1 \lambda_2$ parameter. The $\lambda_1 \lambda_2$ parameter value was calculated for each binned $P(h)$ using a least-squares method, yielding $\lambda_1 \lambda_2 = 2.09$ (Rare), 1.90 (Rare-Clustered), 5.13 (All), and 3.49 (All-Clustered). The inset demonstrates data collapse for all four $P(h/\langle h \rangle)$ distributions following from the universal scaling form of $K_0(x)$.

How do these findings compare with general intuition? Our empirical finding significantly deviates from the prediction which follows from combining Lotka's productivity

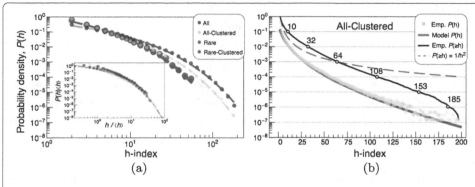

Figure 5 Empirical and theoretical *h*-index distribution. (a) Testing the predictions of a stochastic *h*-index model with empirical data. Shown for each dataset is the empirical probability density function $P(h)$, using logarithmic binning for $h > 10$. We fit each $P(h)$ to the model distribution $P_m(h)$, parametrized by only the distribution average, which is related to the mixing model parameters as $\langle h \rangle = \lambda_1 \lambda_2$. **(Inset)** Data collapse of the empirical distributions along the universal curve $K_0(\sqrt{h}; \lambda_1 \lambda_2 = 1)$ (dashed grey curve) using the scaled variable $x = h/\langle h \rangle$. **(b)** 6,498,286 clusters with $h \geq 2$ were identified for the entire WoS disambiguation. Plotted are the probability distribution $P(h)$ (green circles), the best-fit model $P_m(h)$ with $\lambda_1 \lambda_2 = 3.49$, and the complementary cumulative distribution $P(\geq h)$ (solid black curve). The numbers indicate the value associated with the percentile $100 \times (1 - P(h))$, e.g. 1 per 1,000 clusters (corresponding to the 99.9th percentile) has *h*-index of 64 or greater.

law [24], which states that the number n of publications follows a Pareto power-law distribution $P_p(n) \sim n^{-2}$, and the recent observation that the *h*-index scales as $h \sim n^{1/2}$ [25], which together imply that $P_p(h) \sim h^{-3}$ (corresponding to $P_p(\geq h) = h^{-2}$).

Figure 5(b) compares the empirical complementary cumulative distribution $P(\geq h)$ for both empirical data (representing the 6,498,286 clusters with $h \geq 2$ identified by applying the disambiguation algorithm to the entire WoS dataset) and for the theoretical Pareto distribution $P_p(\geq h) = 1/h^2$. There is a crossover between the two $P(\geq h)$ curves around $h \approx 64$ (corresponding to the 99.9th percentile) which indicates that for $h > 64$ we observe significantly fewer clusters with a given h value than predicted by Lotka's productivity law. For example, the Lotka law predicts a 100-fold increase in the number of scientific profiles with h larger than the 1 per million frequency, $h \geq 185$. This discrepancy likely reflects the finite productivity lifecycle of scientific careers, which is not accounted for in models predicting scale-free Pareto distributions.

So how do these empirical results improve our understanding of how the *h*-index should be used? We show that the sampling bias encountered in small-scale studies [28], and even large-scale studies [25], significantly discounts the frequency of careers with relatively small h. We observe a monotonically decreasing $P(h)$ with a heavy tail, e.g. only 10% of the clusters also have $h \geq 10$. This means that the *h*-index is a noisy comparative metric when h is small since a difference $\delta h \sim 1$ can cause an extremely large change in any ranking between scientists in a realistic academic ranking scenario. Furthermore, our model suggests that disentangling the net *h*-index from its time dependent and discipline dependent factors leads to a more fundamental question: controlling for age and disciplinary factors, what is the distribution of g? Does the distribution of g vary dramatically across age and disciplinary cohorts? This could provide better insight into the interplay between impact, career length [29] and the survival probability of academics [30, 31].

4 Conclusion

The goal of this work was to disambiguate all author names in the WoS database. We found that existing methods relied on metadata that are not available or not complete in WoS, or were not specifically developed for an application to such a huge database. Second, we needed a test dataset which is not limited to certain research fields or geographical regions, and large enough to be representative for WoS. As previous work had shown that even under less demanding conditions perfect disambiguation is not achievable, we concentrated on the most influential work to correctly disambiguate papers that are most cited.

We achieved our goal by disambiguating author names based on the citation graph, which is the main feature of WoS. This approach exploits the fact that, on average, there is much more similarity between two publications written by the same author than between two random publications from different authors who happen to have the same name. We maximized the separation between these two classes, which can be seen as positive or wanted links and unwanted links in a publication network that connects papers written by the same unique researcher. Counting shared outgoing references and incoming citations are a much more fine-grained disambiguation criterion than for example journal or affiliation entries. Our disambiguation method does not assume any specific feature distribution, but is parameterized and trainable according to a suitable "gold standard". It turns out that Google Scholar author profiles, one of the emerging collections of user editable publication lists, can reasonably serve as such a standard.

Our proposed method consists of three main components that could be altered or improved while still keeping the same validation framework: the error measure, the similarity measure and the clustering algorithm. The error measure we presented was specifically developed for reproducing h-indices; we believe other goals could be accomplished as well. The similarity measure could be easily extended by further metadata. Furthermore, our clustering algorithm, while intuitive and computationally efficient, could potentially be replaced by some more sophisticated community detection.

Comparing our results with previous work is difficult, as there is no common benchmark available. There are several studies that analyze small subsets of authors names, which is certainly useful to understand the mechanisms of the respectively proposed algorithms and sometimes unavoidable in lack of a massive test dataset. We realized, however, that this does not allow for generalization across disciplines, time, career age, and varying metadata availability. We also point out that there are differences in the error reporting, mainly in the way how the mean of errors is calculated. The vast majority of authors has only one or two publications, making it likely that the low error rates for precision and recall are underestimated. Some publications report error rates lower than 1-2%. We do not claim such an excellent result, since even our gold standard (cross-referenced publications from Google Scholar profiles, and name initials from WoS) cannot be assumed to have error rates significantly better than that. We have shown instead that using author and citation graph information only, we can disambiguate huge databases in a computationally efficient way and at the same time being flexible regarding the objectives one like to optimize for.

Competing interests
The authors declare that they have no competing interests.

Authors' contributions

DH proposed the citation-network-based name disambiguation approach. CS performed the data analysis. The *h*-index distribution model was developed by AP. The manuscript was written by CS, OP and AP.

Author details

[1]Department of Humanities and Social Sciences, Chair of Sociology, in particular of Modeling and Simulation, ETH Zurich, Clausiusstrasse 50, CH-8092 Zurich, Switzerland. [2]IMT Institute for Advanced Studies Lucca, Piazza San Francesco 19, 55100 Lucca, Italy.

Acknowledgements

The authors would like to thank Tobias Kuhn and Michael Maes for useful feedback. This work was inspired by the FuturICT project, in particular its part on the Innovation Accelerator. OP acknowledges funding from the Social Sciences and Humanities Research Council of Canada. We acknowledge Thomson ISI as required by the terms of use of our WoS data license.

References

1. Smalheiser NR, Torvik VI (2009) Author name disambiguation. Annu Rev Inf Sci Technol 43(1):1-43
2. Ferreira AA, Gonçalves MA, Laender AH (2012) A brief survey of automatic methods for author name disambiguation. SIGMOD Rec 41(2):15-26
3. Mazloumian A, Helbing D, Lozano S, Light RP, Börner K (2013) Global multi-level analysis of the 'scientific food web'. Sci Rep 3:1167
4. Radicchi F (2012) In science "there is no bad publicity": papers criticized in comments have high scientific impact. Sci Rep 2:815
5. Larivière V, Ni C, Gingras Y, Cronin B, Sugimoto CR (2013) Global gender disparities in science. Nature 504(7479):211-213
6. Mazloumian A, Eom Y-H, Helbing D, Lozano S, Fortunato S (2011) How citation boosts promote scientific paradigm shifts and Nobel prizes. PLoS ONE 6(5):18975
7. Petersen AM, Fortunato S, Pan RK, Kaski K, Penner O, Rungi A, Riccaboni M, Stanley HE, Pammolli F (2014) Reputation and impact in academic careers. Proc Natl Acad Sci USA. doi:10.1073/pnas.1323111111
8. Fleming L, Sorenson O (2004) Science as a map in technological search. Strateg Manag J 25(8-9):909-928
9. Fleming L, Mingo S, Chen D (2007) Collaborative brokerage, generative creativity, and creative success. Adm Sci Q 52(3):443-475
10. Acuna DE, Allesina S, Kording KP (2012) Predicting scientific success. Nature 489(7415):201-202
11. Mazloumian A (2012) Predicting scholars' scientific impact. PLoS ONE 7(11):49246
12. Penner O, Petersen AM, Pan RK, Fortunato S (2013) Commentary: the case for caution in predicting scientists' future impact. Phys Today 66(4):8-9
13. Penner O, Pan RK, Petersen AM, Fortunato S (2013) On the predictability of future impact in science. Sci Rep 3:3052
14. Acuna DE, Penner O, Orton CG (2013) Point/counterpoint: the future *h*-index is an excellent way to predict scientists' future impact. Med Phys 40(11):110601
15. ORCID (2013) Open researcher and contributor ID. www.orcid.org. Accessed 12 Aug 2013
16. VIVO (2013) VIVO. www.vivoweb.org. Accessed 12 Aug 2013
17. Torvik VI, Weeber M, Swanson DR, Smalheiser NR (2005) A probabilistic similarity metric for medline records: a model for author name disambiguation. J Am Soc Inf Sci Technol 56(2):140-158
18. Torvik VI, Smalheiser NR (2009) Author name disambiguation in medline. ACM Trans Knowl Discov Data 3(3):11
19. Levin M, Krawczyk S, Bethard S, Jurafsky D (2012) Citation-based bootstrapping for large-scale author disambiguation. J Am Soc Inf Sci Technol 63(5):1030-1047
20. Tang L, Walsh JP (2010) Bibliometric fingerprints: name disambiguation based on approximate structure equivalence of cognitive maps. Scientometrics 84:763-784
21. D'Angelo CA, Giuffrida C, Abramo G (2011) A heuristic approach to author name disambiguation in bibliometrics databases for large-scale research assessments. J Am Soc Inf Sci Technol 62(2):257-269
22. Reijnhoudt L, Costas R, Noyons E, Boerner K, Scharnhorst A (2013) "seed + expand": a validated methodology for creating high quality publication oeuvres of individual researchers. In: Proceedings of ISSI 2013 – 14th international society of scientometrics and informetrics conference. arXiv:1301.5177
23. ANVUR (2013) National Agency for the Evaluation of Universities and Research Institutes (Italy). http://www.anvur.org/attachments/article/253/normalizzazione_indicatori_0.pdf. Accessed 17 Sep 2014
24. Lotka AJ (1926) The frequency distribution of scientific productivity. J Wash Acad Sci 16(12):317-323
25. Radicchi F, Castellano C (2013) Analysis of bibliometric indicators for individual scholars in a large data set. Scientometrics 97:627-637
26. Hellsten I, Lambiotte R, Scharnhorst A, Ausloos M (2007) Self-citations, co-authorships and keywords: a new approach to scientists' field mobility? Scientometrics 72(3):469-486
27. Salton G (1968) Automatic information organization and retrieval
28. Hirsch J (2005) An index to quantify an individual's scientific research output. Proc Natl Acad Sci USA 102:16569-16572
29. Petersen AM, Jung W-S, Yang J-S, Stanley HE (2011) Quantitative and empirical demonstration of the Matthew effect in a study of career longevity. Proc Natl Acad Sci USA 108(1):18-23
30. Kaminski D, Geisler C (2012) Survival analysis of faculty retention in science and engineering by gender. Science 335:864-866
31. Petersen AM, Riccaboni M, Stanley HE, Pammolli F (2012) Persistence and uncertainty in the academic career. Proc Natl Acad Sci USA 109:5213-5218

3

Stock fluctuations are correlated and amplified across networks of interlocking directorates

Serguei Saavedra[1*], Luis J Gilarranz[1], Rudolf P Rohr[1,2], Michael Schnabel[3,4], Brian Uzzi[3,4] and Jordi Bascompte[1]

*Correspondence:
serguei.saavedra@ebd.csic.es
[1]Integrative Ecology Group,
Estación Biológica de Doñana
(EBD-CSIC), Calle Américo Vespucio
s/n, Sevilla, 41092, Spain
Full list of author information is
available at the end of the article

Abstract

Traded corporations are required by law to have a majority of outside directors on their board. This requirement allows the existence of directors who sit on the board of two or more corporations at the same time, generating what is commonly known as interlocking directorates. While research has shown that networks of interlocking directorates facilitate the transmission of information between corporations, little is known about the extent to which such interlocking networks can explain the fluctuations of stock price returns. Yet, this is a special concern since the risk of amplifying stock fluctuations is latent. To answer this question, here we analyze the board composition, traders' perception, and stock performance of more than 1,500 US traded corporations from 2007-2011. First, we find that the fewer degrees of separation between two corporations in the interlocking network, the stronger the temporal correlation between their stock price returns. Second, we find that the centrality of traded corporations in the interlocking network correlates with the frequency at which financial traders talk about such corporations, and this frequency is in turn proportional to the corresponding traded volume. Third, we show that the centrality of corporations was negatively associated with their stock performance in 2008, the year of the big financial crash. These results suggest that the strategic decisions made by interlocking directorates are strongly followed by stock analysts and have the potential to correlate and amplify the movement of stock prices during financial crashes. These results may have relevant implications for scholars, investors, and regulators.

Keywords: stock market; corporate governance; interlocking networks; information transmission; financial traders

1 Introduction

According to corporate governance standards in the US [1], traded corporations are required to have a minimum of three directors in their board and a majority of outside directors [2, 3]. Typically, these outside directors either have their primary affiliation with a different corporation, are self-employed, or retired [2]. This allows a director to sit on the board of two or more corporations at the same time - including or not their own affiliation board, generating what is commonly known as interlocking directorates [2–5]. In turn, interlocking networks emerge as the result of many interconnected interlocking directorates [2, 3]. Indeed, interlocking networks have been the focus of numerous research analyzing their role in the performance of corporations, organizational failure, economic downturns, hegemony, CEO pay, the sale price of a corporation, stock synchronicity, and prices for a corporation's services, among others [2, 3, 6–10]. Yet, the strongest consensus so far is that interlocking networks mainly favor the transmission of information among corporations [3, 5, 11]. For instance, this information advantage has been observed when central corporations of interlocking networks can adopt new market strategies quicker via information they gather from their interlocking directorates [12, 13].

A major question that remains to be answered is whether interlocking networks can affect market processes [3]. Board members are typically major stockholders and report financial strategies to their investors [2, 3]. Indeed, previous work has suggested that interlocking directorates may play an important role in the information gathered by stock analysts, especially when there is substantial media coverage [14]. This is a special concern of regulators since the risk of amplifying stock fluctuations is latent [2, 3]. In fact, this question has motivated important actions in the US Congress dating back to the early 1900's [2]. Section 8 of the Clayton Act explicitly prohibited interlocks if the linked corporations would violate antitrust laws if combined into a single corporation [2, 4]. Over the years, these actions have promoted a decrease in the number of interlocking directorates, especially within the financial sector [3]. However, even with these limitations, it has been shown that financial shocks can be transmitted across the interlocking network regardless of the degrees of separation between corporations [2, 3, 15–17].

To shed new light on the above question, we study the extent to which interlocking networks can explain stock fluctuations. We analyze data on the board composition, traders' perception, and stock performance of more than 1,500 US traded corporations (see the Appendix for further details). To capture the behavior of interlocking networks across a variety of financial periods, we focus our analysis on the period covered by the big 2008 financial crash and its pre and post financial periods. We use the data extracted from *RiskMetrics* [18], which is a yearly compilation from 2007-2011 of the board composition of over 1,500 large US traded corporations. Daily closing stock prices for these corporations are extracted from *WRDS* database [19], and stocks are categorized in a market sector according to *Yahoo Finance* criteria [20]. We analyze traders' perception on these traded corporations using trading data and electronic communication among traders from one US trading firm for the period 2007-2009 [21, 22]. Here, we explore the extent to which interlocking networks can explain stock correlations, the plausible mechanisms linking interlocking networks and stock markets, and the potential effect of such associations.

2 Results
2.1 Network characterization
We constructed interlocking networks for each year from 2007-2011 formed only by the traded corporations observed in a particular year. A link between two corporations is established if they share at least one board member in the same year. Consistent with previous studies and regulations [2, 3], we find that the observed boards in these interlocking networks have a median size of 9 directors, of which the majority are outside directors (>50%). The 99% of the observed interlocking directorates (i.e., links between two corporations) share only one board member. In total, there is approximately 20% of corporations who do not share any single director with another corporation, whereas the other 80% are

on average 4.6 interlocking directorates apart from each other. Interestingly, 85% of all interlocking directorates are formed between corporations that belong to different market sectors, and we find no significant connectivity differences across market sectors. These results are also in agreement with the characterization of interlocking networks found in previous studies [16, 17].

Whereas the characterization of the interlocking network remains fairly constant across the observation period, the financial market exhibited important fluctuations from year to year. In 2007, 46% of the 1,422 observed traded corporations increased their stock price by the end of the year. In contrast, in 2008, the year of the big financial crash, only 12% of the 1,453 observed traded corporations increased their stock price. This was followed by a recovery period in 2009 and 2010 were 81% of 1,357 and 1,413 observed corporations increased their stock price, respectively. Finally, in 2011, the market had a relatively bad period with 41% of 1,447 observed corporations increasing their stock price. Therefore, these data bring us the opportunity to investigate the association between interlocking networks and stock fluctuations across different financial periods.

2.2 Interlocking networks and stock correlations

To study whether stock correlations can follow a characteristic pattern among interlocking directorates, we measure the association between network proximity - degrees of separation - and market similarity - temporal correlation of stock prices - among traded corporations (Figure 1). It was previously shown that the synchronicity between two stocks can

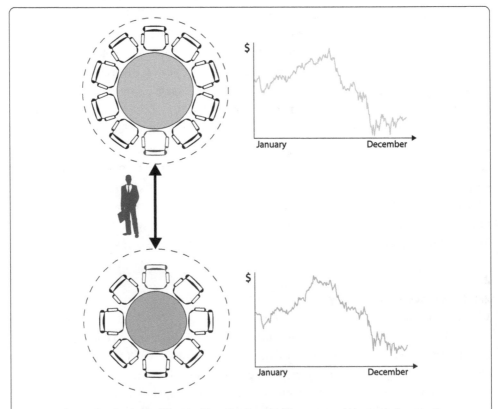

Figure 1 Illustrative example of interlocking directorates. The green and blue traded corporations are linked by their inside/outside director that sits on their board. The question is whether traded corporations that are closer in the interlocking network also have a stronger correlation between their stocks.

increase if these two corporations share a director [10]. Here, we expand on this question to ask whether traded corporations that are closer in the interlocking network also have a stronger correlation between their stocks. For each year, we define a matrix of network proximity **D** of size $N \times N$, where N is the number of observed traded corporations in a year, $D_{ij} = 1/(d_{ij})$, and d_{ij} is the degree of separation (number of links) between corporation i and j in the interlocking network. Note that the degree of separation of a corporation to itself is $d_{ii} = 0$, and unconnected corporations have an infinite degree of separation ($d_{ij} = \infty$). The greater D_{ij}, the higher the proximity between the two corporations in the interlocking network. Note that our matrix of network proximity takes into account all pairs of traded corporations.

Additionally, we define a matrix of market similarity $\mathbf{S} = \frac{1}{M-1}RR^{T}$ of size $N \times N$, where M is the total number of trading days in a year, and $R_{ik} = (z_{ik} - \langle z_{ik} \rangle)/\sigma_{z_{ik}}$ is the standard deviation normalized daily log returns of stock i in day k such that $z_{ik} = \log(p_i(k)/p_i(k-1))$ and $p_i(k)$ is the closing stock price of corporation i in day k. Therefore, the matrix of market similarity **S** corresponds to the correlation matrix Σ_R of R [23]. The higher S_{ij}, the higher the similarity or temporal correlation of the stock price movements of corporation i and j in the year.

We calculate partial Mantel correlations [24] (both Spearman and Pearson correlations) between the matrices of network proximity and market similarity while controlling for other proximity matrices given by market sector, geographic distance, board size, fraction of directors with financial expertise, and average stock price in the year (see the Appendix for further details). Following previous studies [25–29], we use the average stock price in the year as surrogate of firm size given its relevance and undisputed effect on the analysis of stock fluctuations. We also divide our analysis into the biggest market sectors (Basic Materials, Consumer Goods, Financial, Health Care, Industrial Goods, Services, and Technology), where sector matrices are simply sub-matrices of the full proximity matrices composed of corporations from a single sector.

Importantly, we find positive correlations between network proximity and market similarity in both individual sectors and in the market as a whole (i.e., taking all sectors together). Figure 2 shows that the majority (23 out of 35, $P = 0.024$, binomial test) of partial Mantel correlations yield positive correlations with 95% bootstrap confidence intervals (solid circles). These correlations hold to additional non-parametric statistical tests (see

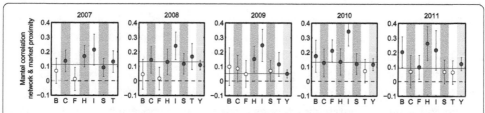

Figure 2 Interlocking networks and stock correlations. Spearman partial Mantel correlations (Pearson correlations yield similar results) between the matrices of network proximity and market similarity of traded corporations in each year. The red/solid line corresponds to the calculated correlation for all traded corporations regardless of market sector. Circles correspond to correlations in a particular market sector. Solid symbols correspond to correlations that do not cross zero using bootstrap 95% confidence intervals (error bars). We focus on the seven major sectors: (B) basic materials, (C) consumer goods, (F) financial, (H) healthcare, (I) industrial, (S) services, and (T) technology. The Y column in 2008-2011 corresponds to the correlation between changes in network proximity and changes in market similarity for all pairs of traded corporations in reference to their values in the previous year.

the Appendix). While the correlations found have relatively small values (the largest is 0.4), let us not forget that even small changes in the price of stocks can generate big losses or gains in the market [22, 30]. Moreover, these correlation values are larger than the values generated if we only focus on distances $d_{ij} = 1$ (see the Appendix), following previous work [10]. Interestingly, we can also observe that not all sector behave in the same way. For instance, the interlocking networks of the healthcare and industrial sectors can explain more clearly the stock correlations among their constituent traded corporations than the consumer or financial sector. We can also see that some sectors, such as the financial or technological sector, change from negligible (positive) correlations at the beginning of the observational period to positive (negligible) correlations by the end of the period. We leave future explanations of these changes to the reader.

To further support the validity of the correlations between network proximity and market similarity, we test whether corporations that increase or decrease their network proximity from one year to the next one also increase or decrease their market similarity accordingly. In specific, for each year from 2008-2011, we calculate a new matrix of network proximity given by the difference between the network proximity between two corporations in a given year $D_{ij}(t)$ and their network proximity in the previous year $D_{ij}(t-1)$ (only taking into account those corporations that are present in both years). Similarly, we generate a new matrix of market similarity for each year from 2008-2011, in which the new elements of each of these matrices are given by the difference between the market similarity between two corporations in a given year $S_{ij}(t)$ and their market similarity in the previous year $S_{ij}(t-1)$. Finally, for each year, we measure the correlation between the newly generated matrices of network proximity and market similarity.

Figure 2 (green/Y region) shows that the new correlations between proximity changes are, in fact, equivalent to the positive correlations in each year. Overall, these findings reveal that changes in the degree of separation between two corporations in the interlocking network are correlated with changes in their stock correlations. If the degree of separation decreases, the stock correlation increases, and vice versa.

2.3 Interlocking networks and stock markets

To unveil potential mechanisms explaining the previous association between stock correlations and interlocking networks, we study the behavior of one the main financial actors towards interlocking directorates. In specific, we analyze the perception and information gathered by stock analysts on traded corporations and whether this is associated with their trading activity. As proxy for the information collected by stock analysts, we use trading data and the electronic communication among a group of financial traders from a US trading company from 2007-2009 (see the Appendix). Previous work has revealed that traders are constantly tracking business press coverage of traded corporations and exchanging this information among their peers [21]. An illustrative example of this information concerning corporate directorates is the following message between two traders on July 7th 2008: 'Microsoft willing to enter talks if Yahoo elects new board.' In fact, it has been shown that traders' communications can signal their understanding of market volatility [21, 22]. Therefore, this suggests that the more strategic decisions made by interlocking directorates, the higher the chances that there is a media coverage of relevance to traders, and the higher the potential that this correlates with their trading activity.

To test the above hypothesis, for each year from 2007-2009, we investigate the association of the frequency at which traders talk about traded corporations with the centrality

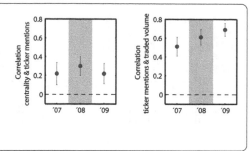

Figure 3 Interlocking networks and stock markets. For each year from 2007-2009, the figure shows Spearman rank correlations (Pearson correlations yield similar results) between tickers' mentions and the centrality of such corporations in the interlocking network. Similarly, the figure shows Spearman rank correlations (Pearson correlations yield similar results) between tickers' mentions and the traded volume of such corporations by the same group of traders over the entire year.

in the interlocking network and the traded volume of such corporations. The frequency is calculated by the total number of times a ticker (e.g. GOOG as for Google) is mentioned over the entire year by this group of traders. We measure a corporation's centrality by $\langle D_i \rangle = \frac{1}{N-1} \sum_j D_{ij}$, where D_{ij} is the network proximity between two corporations, as mentioned above. We find that similar results are obtained if we replace $\langle D_i \rangle$ by other centrality measures, such as the total number of interlocking directors or the community participation coefficient [31]. The traded volume is calculated by the total amount of US dollars traded by this group of traders over the entire year.

Figure 3 shows indeed a positive association (partial Spearman rank correlation) of ticker mentions with both the centrality and traded volume of corporations, controlling for the average stock price, board size, and fraction of financial experts in the board. Interestingly, we find negligible associations (partial Spearman rank correlation) between centrality and traded volume, controlling for ticker mentions, the average stock price, board size, and fraction of financial experts in the board. This supports the hypothesis of a path going from interlocking directorates to traders reacting to information and then to trading activity. Overall, these findings show an enhanced attention of stock analysts to central corporations in interlocking networks.

2.4 Exposure to market fluctuations in interlocking networks

Finally, to test the extent to which interlocking networks can amplify the exposure of traded corporations to market fluctuations, we compare the centrality of corporations in the interlocking network with their stock performance over the year. The centrality of a corporations is again measured by $\langle D_i \rangle$. We measure a corporation's short-term and long-term stock performance by its beta (β_i) and its yearly stock price return (r_i), respectively.

The commonly known beta of a stock is given by $\beta_i = \mathrm{Cov}(z_i, z_b) / \mathrm{Var}(z_b)$, where z_i and z_b are the daily log returns of stocks i and the benchmark return, respectively (see the Appendix). The higher (lower) the beta, the more the stock moves in the same (opposite) direction and farther apart from the benchmark return. This means that during good or bad market periods, the short-term stock performance of a traded corporation increases the higher or the lower the beta of the stock, respectively. The yearly stock price return is given by $r_i = \log(p_i(t_f)/p_i(t_o))$, where $p_i(t_o)$ and $p_i(t_f)$ are the daily closing stock prices of corporation i at the beginning and at the end of the calendar year, respectively. The higher the yearly return, the better the long-term stock performance of a traded corporation. For each year from 2007-2011, we measure the effect of centrality on the short-term and long-term stock performance using a multivariate linear regression model controlling for the corporations' individual characteristics (see the Appendix).

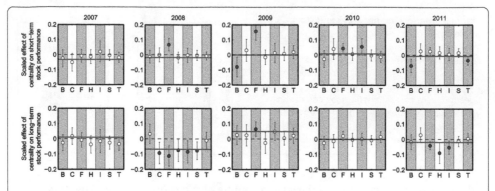

Figure 4 Exposure of traded corporations to market fluctuations. The first row corresponds to the scaled effect of centrality of traded corporations on their short-term stock performance - beta of stocks. The second row corresponds to the scaled effect of centrality of traded corporations on their long-term stock performance - yearly log returns of stocks. The red/solid line corresponds to the effect when taking into account all traded corporations regardless of market sector. Circles correspond to effects in a particular market sector. Solid symbols correspond to effects that do not cross zero using bootstrap 95% confidence intervals (error bars). We focus on the seven major sectors: (B) basic materials, (C) consumer goods, (F) financial, (H) healthcare, (I) industrial, (S) services, and (T) technology.

In general, Figure 4 shows that the centrality of traded corporations has negligible effects on their long-term and short-term stock performance (but see the Financial sector). This is in line with our previous findings showing that interlocking networks favor stock correlations and, in turn, this may explain why interlocking networks have no effect on pushing traded corporations away from the general market trend. However, Figure 4 also reveals that during 2008, the year of the big financial crash, there is a negative effect between centrality and long-term stock performance. These results suggest that during financial crashes, interlocking networks can amplify the exposure of traded corporations to market fluctuations.

3 Discussion

US governance standards favor the participation of outside directors in corporate boards, which in turn allows the creation of interlocking directorates. While direct competitors are prohibited to create interlocking directorates, these corporations have on average only four degrees of separation. The financial sector is a good example of this market environment. There is almost no interlocking directorate between financial corporations, but they are indirectly linked by their interlocking directors sitting on the board of a third corporation belonging to a different market sector. Indeed, as we mentioned before, 85% of interlocking directorates are formed between corporations belonging to different market sectors. While interlocking networks facilitate the transmission of information, it has been unclear whether they can also explain stock fluctuations in the financial market.

Our findings have shown that interlocking directorates seem to be one of the factors favoring the existence of stock correlations. We acknowledge that other confounding factors can explain stock correlations. Interestingly, a potential mechanism explaining the link between interlocking networks and stock markets appears to be the enhanced attention of stock analysts to central corporations. It remains to be seen whether other measures of centrality can provide better insights about these associations. Importantly, because interlocking networks may amplify market fluctuations during financial crashes, future work should also explore the impact of the different dynamics found across market sectors. Importantly, it does not escape our notice that these results provide valuable non-opinionated insight for scholars, regulators, investors, and board members themselves.

Appendix
Board composition data

We use the data extracted from *RiskMetrics* [18], which is a yearly compilation from 2007-2011 of the board composition of over 1,500 large US traded corporations. We use only those traded corporation on which we could find stock price information in our stock price data. Board members were manually disambiguated using gender, age, and affiliation data provided by *RiskMetrics*. These data also have information of whether a board member is consider a financial expert by the traded corporation. In some cases, the same board member is classified as a financial member in one corporations but a non-financial expert in a second corporation. We decided to classify board members as financial experts if they are considered to be experts at least in one corporation. The board composition and their financial expertise for each year is provided in Additional file 1.

Stock price data

Daily closing stock prices from 2007-2011 for these corporations are extracted from *WRDS* database [19], and stocks are categorized in a market sector according to *Yahoo Finance* criteria [20]. The stock data and market classification for each year is provided in Additional file 1.

Traders data

Our data includes the full population of more than 3 million instant messages sent/received and more than 1 million of trading decisions of day traders at a typical small-to-medium sized US trading company from 2007-2009. All trading related data was automatically captured by the company's trading system, which is specially designed for accuracy in recording, and used by most other companies in the industry. The study conforms to Institutional Review Board (IRB) criteria. There was no subject interaction, all data was 100% archival, and the company and the subjects were anonymized. Legally, all data used in the study is owned by the company. All traders at the company know the company owns the data and that their communications and trading behavior is recorded by law. We received written permission from the company to use these data for research purposes and publishing contingent on identifying characteristics of the company and its traders remaining confidential and anonymous. For further details see Refs. [21, 22]. We use only those tickers that we were able to disambiguate across traders' communications. Tickers' mentions and traded volume are normalized (to preserve the company's confidentiality) and provided in Additional file 1.

Control proximity matrices

Partial Mantel correlations between network proximity and market similarity are controlled by proximity in market sector F, average stock price in the year T, board size B, fraction of directors with financial expertise E, and geographic distance G. The proximity matrix F corresponds to $F_{i,j} = 1$ if traded corporation i and j belong to the same sector, 0 otherwise. In the rest of the control proximity matrices, the elements (i, j) of these matrices correspond to the inverse of the normalized absolute differences between the value measured in corporation i and j, such that higher values always represent corporations with higher proximity. For proximity matrix $\mathbf{T}$, $T_{ij} = (\max\{k1\} - k1_{ij})/(\max\{k1\} - \min\{k1\})$ where $k1_{ij} = |\langle \log(p_i) \rangle - \langle \log(p_j) \rangle|$ and $\langle \log(p_i) \rangle$ is the average log price of stock i over the year. For proximity matrix $\mathbf{B}$, $B_{ij} = (\max\{k2\} - k2_{ij})/(\max\{k2\} - \min\{k2\})$ where $k2_{ij} = |b_i - b_j|$ and b_i is the total number of board members of traded corporation i over the year. For proximity matrix $\mathbf{E}$, $E_{ij} = (\max\{k3\} - k3_{ij})/(\max\{k3\} - \min\{k3\})$ where $k3_{ij} = |e_i - e_j|$ and e_i is the fraction of board members with financial expertise of traded corporation i over the year. For proximity matrix $\mathbf{G}$, $G_{ij} = (\max\{k4\} - k4_{ij})/(\max\{k4\} - \min\{k4\})$ where $k4_{ij}$ is the geographic distance between corporation i and j as function of their geographic coordinates latitude and longitude extracted from their zip codes. Zip codes were collected from *Yahoo Finance* and from *HighBeam.Com*. These data are provided in Additional file 1. We find a majority of negligible associations of market similarity with the control proximity matrices of firm size, board size, fraction of financial experts in the board, and geographic distance (see Figures S1-S4 in Additional file 2).

Robustness of correlations between network proximity and market similarity

We find that each of the positive correlations shown in Figure 2 is also higher than the expected correlation between network proximity and market similarity when we randomly generate new matrices of network proximity (see Figure S5 in Additional file 2). These new matrices are generated by bootstrapping elements with replacement from the original matrices of network proximity. Additionally, the observed correlations between network proximity and market similarity shown in Figure 2 cannot be reproduced if we disconnect boards (i.e., $d_{ij} = \infty$) when a certain degree of separation has been exceed (see Figure S6 in Additional file 2).

Benchmark return

To calculate the benchmark return, we use the average daily log returns $z_b = \langle z_i \rangle$ of all the observed corporations. For individual market sectors, we did not find statistical differences if we use $\langle z_i \rangle$ or the average daily stock returns only of corporations from individual market sectors. The distribution of betas and yearly stock returns are shown in Figure S7 in Additional file 2.

Multivariate linear regression model

The model is defined by *performance*$_i \sim \langle D_i \rangle + \langle \log(p_i) \rangle + b_i + f_i + \epsilon_i$. The response variable *performance* can take either the beta of the stock β_i or the yearly stock return r_i. We control for the average price of the stocks in the year ($\langle \log(p_i) \rangle$), the size of the boards (b_i), the fraction of directors with financial expertise in each board (f_i), and the Gaussian noise (ϵ_i). We scale all predictor variables to be able to compare their effect. The model has a goodness-of-fit of $R^2 \sim 0.3$ for all years. Interestingly, the control variables board size and fraction of directors with financial expertise show a majority of negligible effects, while firm size yields positive and negative effects for short-term and long-term stock performance (see Figures S8-S10 in Additional file 2).

Mantel correlation

This correlation is the extension of the standard Pearson or Spearman rank correlation to dyadic data [24]. Mantel correlation works as follows, let us assume that we have two sets of n objects represented by their similarity matrices X_{ij} and Y_{ij}, i.e., dyadic data. For example in our case, network proximity and market similarity. The Pearson Mantel correlation coefficient is computed as

$$r = \frac{\sum_{i>j}(X_{ij} - \bar{X})(Y_{ij} - \bar{Y})}{\sum_{i>j}(X_{ij} - \bar{X})^2 \sum_{i>j}(Y_{ij} - \bar{Y})^2},$$

where $\bar{X} = \frac{2}{n(n-1)}\sum_{i>j} X_{ij}$ is the average Xij value (similarly for $\bar{Y}$). Note that the sum is only made on the strictly upper triangular part of the matrices. This is so because similarity matrices are symmetric and have their diagonal elements equal to one. For the Spearman rank Mantel correlation, we first substitute the elements of the matrices X_{ij} and Y_{ij} by their respective rank. In a similar way we can compute partial Mantel correlations [32]. To compute the 95% confidence interval of the correlation coefficient, we use a bootstrap procedure [33]. We re-sample simultaneously the rows and the columns of the similarity matrices, and then for each re-sampling we compute again the Mantel correlation coefficient. The re-sampling procedure results in the empirical distribution of the Mantel correlation coefficient, from which we extract the 95% confidence interval.

Additional material

Additional file 1: Additional data.
Additional file 2: Additional figures.

Competing interests
The authors declare no competing financial interests.

Authors' contributions
All authors contributed extensively to the work presented in this paper.

Author details
[1]Integrative Ecology Group, Estación Biológica de Doñana (EBD-CSIC), Calle Américo Vespucio s/n, Sevilla, 41092, Spain. [2]Unit of Ecology and Evolution, Department of Biology, University of Fribourg, Chemin du Musée 10, Fribourg, 1700, Switzerland. [3]Northwestern Institute on Complex Systems, Northwestern University, Evanston, Illinois 60208, USA. [4]Kellogg School of Management, Northwestern University, Evanston, Illinois 60208, USA.

Acknowledgements
Funding was provided by the European Research Council through an Advanced Grant (JB), the Spanish Ministry of Education through a FPU PhD Fellowship (LJG), FP7-REGPOT-2010-1 program under project 264125 EcoGenes (RPR), and the Kellogg School of Management (MS).

References
1. http://nysemanual.nyse.com/lcm/ (2013)
2. Mizruchi MS (1996) What do interlocks do? An analysis, critique, and assessment of research on interlocking directorates. Annu Rev Sociol 22:271-298
3. Burt RS (2006) Interlocking directorates behind the S&P indices. School of Business, Chicago. http://faculty.chicagobooth.edu/ronald.burt/research/IDS&P.pdf
4. Dooley PC (1969) The interlocking directorate. Am Econ Rev 59:314-323
5. Carpenter MA, Westphal JD (2001) The strategic context of external network ties: examining the impact of director appointments on board involvement in strategic decision making. Acad Manag J 4:639-660
6. Pennings JM (1980) Interlocking directorates. Jossey-Bass, San Francisco
7. Palmer D, Barber BM, Zhou X (1995) The finance conception of control: the theory that ate New York? Reply to Fligstein. Am Sociol Rev 60:504-508
8. Fligstein N, Brantley P (1992) Bank control, owner control, or organizational dynamics: who controls the large modern corporation? Am J Sociol 98:280-307
9. Fligstein N (1995) Networks of power of the finance conception of control? Comment on Palmer, Barber, Zhou, and Soysal. Am Sociol Rev 60:500-503
10. Khanna T, Thomas C (2009) Synchronicity and firm interlocks in an emerging market. J Financ Econ 92:182-204

11. Borgatti SP, Cross R (2003) A relational view of information seeking and learning in social networks. Manag Sci 49:432-445
12. Connelly BL, Johnson JL, Tihanyi L, Ellstrand AE (2011) More than adopters: competing influences in the interlocking directorate. Organ Sci 22:688-703
13. Davis GF (1991) Agents without principles? The spread of the poison pill through the intercorporate network. Adm Sci Q 36:583-613
14. Haunschild PR, Beckman CM (1998) When do interlocks matter?: Alternate sources of information and interlock influence. Adm Sci Q 43:815-844
15. Vedres B (1997) The constellation of economic power: the position of political actors, banks, and large corporations in the network of directorate interlock in Hungary. Int Netw Soc Netw Anal 23:44-59
16. Kogut B, Walker G (2001) The small world of Germany and the durability of national networks. Am Sociol Rev 66:317-335
17. Battiston S, Bonaneau E, Weisbuch G (2003) Decision making dynamics in corporate boards. Physica A 322:567
18. http://wrds-web.wharton.upenn.edu/wrds/ds/riskmetrics/rmdirectors/index.cfm (September 2013)
19. http://wrds-web.wharton.upenn.edu/wrds/ (September 2013)
20. http://biz.yahoo.com/p/s_conamed.html (September 2013)
21. Saavedra S, Duch J, Uzzi B (2011) Tracking traders' understanding of the market using e-communication data. PLoS ONE 6:e26705
22. Saavedra S, Malmgren RD, Switanek N, Uzzi B (2013) Foraging under conditions of short-term exploitative competition: the case of stock traders. Proc R Soc Lond B 280:20122901
23. Fenn DJ, Porter MA, Williams S, McDonald M, Johnson NF, Jones NS (2011) Temporal evolution of financial market correlations. Phys Rev E 84:026109
24. Mantel N (1967) The detection of disease clustering and a generalized regression approach. Cancer Res 27:209-220
25. Banz RW (1981) The relationship between return and market value of common stocks. J Financ Econ 9:3-18
26. Schwert GW (1983) Size and stock returns, and other empirical regularities. J Financ Econ 12:3-12
27. Cheung YW, Ng LK (1992) Stock price dynamics and firm size: an empirical investigation. J Finance 47:1985-1997
28. Davis LJ (1994) The cross-section of realized stock returns: the pre-COMPUSTAT evidence. J Finance 49:1579-1593
29. Berk JB (1995) A critique of size-related anomalies. Rev Financ Stud 8:275-286
30. Moro E, Vicente J, Moyano LG, Gerig A, Farmer JD, Vaglica G, Lillo F, Mantegna RN (2009) Market impact and trading profile of hidden orders in stock markets. Phys Rev E 80:e066102
31. Guimerá R, Amaral LAN (2005) Functional cartography of complex metabolic networks. Nature 433:895-900
32. Legendre P (2000) Comparison of permutation methods for the partial correlation and partial mantel test. J Stat Comput Simul 67:37-73
33. Bradley E, Tibshirani RJ (1994) An introduction to the bootstrap. Chapman & Hall/CRC, Boca Raton

4

Privacy-by-design in big data analytics and social mining

Anna Monreale[1,2]*, Salvatore Rinzivillo[2], Francesca Pratesi[1,2], Fosca Giannotti[2] and Dino Pedreschi[1]

*Correspondence:
annam@di.unipi.it
[1] Department of Computer Science,
University of Pisa, Largo Pontecorvo,
3, Pisa, Italy
[2] ISTI-CNR, Via G. Moruzzi, 1, Pisa,
Italy

Abstract

Privacy is ever-growing concern in our society and is becoming a fundamental aspect to take into account when one wants to use, publish and analyze data involving human personal sensitive information. Unfortunately, it is increasingly hard to transform the data in a way that it protects sensitive information: we live in the era of big data characterized by unprecedented opportunities to sense, store and analyze social data describing human activities in great detail and resolution. As a result, privacy preservation simply cannot be accomplished by de-identification alone. In this paper, we propose the *privacy-by-design* paradigm to develop technological frameworks for countering the threats of undesirable, unlawful effects of privacy violation, without obstructing the knowledge discovery opportunities of social mining and big data analytical technologies. Our main idea is to inscribe privacy protection into the knowledge discovery technology by design, so that the analysis incorporates the relevant privacy requirements from the start.

Keywords: privacy-by-design; bid data analytics; social mining

1 Introduction

The big data originating from the digital breadcrumbs of human activities, sensed as a by-product of the ICT systems that we use everyday, record the multiple dimensions of social life: automated payment systems record the tracks of our purchases; search engines record the logs of our queries for finding information on the web; social networking services record our connections to friends, colleagues and collaborators; wireless networks and mobile devices record the traces of our movements. These kinds of big data describing human activities are at the heart of the idea of a 'knowledge society', where the understanding of social phenomena is sustained by the knowledge extracted from the miners of big data across the various social dimensions by using social mining technologies. Thus, the analysis of our digital traces can create new opportunities to understand complex aspects, such as mobility behaviors [1–7], economic and financial crises, the spread of epidemics [8–11], the diffusion of opinions [12] and so on.

The worrying side of this story is that this big data contain personal sensitive information, so that the opportunities of discovering knowledge increase with the risks of privacy violation. When personal sensitive data are published and/or analyzed, one important question to consider is whether this may violate the privacy right of individuals. The human data may potentially reveal many facets of the private life of a person: but a higher level of danger is reached if the various forms of data can be linked together. It is evident that maintaining control on personal data guaranteeing privacy protection is increasingly difficult and it cannot simply be accomplished by de-identification [13] (i.e., by removing the direct identifiers contained in the data). Many examples of re-identification from supposedly anonymous data have been reported in the scientific literature and in the media, from health records to querylogs to GPS trajectories.

In the past few years, several techniques have been proposed to develop technological frameworks for countering privacy violations, without losing the benefits of big data analytics technology [14–18]. Despite these efforts, no general method exists that is capable of handling both generic personal data and preserving generic analytical results. Anonymity in generic sense is considered a chimera and the concern about intrusion in the private sphere by means of big data is now in news headlines of major media. Nevertheless, big data analytics and privacy are not necessary enemies. The purpose of this paper is precisely to show that many practical and impactful services based on big data analytics can be designed in such a way that the quality of results can coexist with high protection of personal data. The magic word is privacy-by-design. We propose here a methodology for purpose-driven privacy protection, where the purpose is a target knowledge service to be deployed on top of data analysis. The basic observation is that providing a reasonable trade-off between a measurable protection of individual privacy together with a measurable quality of service is unfeasible in general, but it becomes feasible in context, i.e., in reference to the kind of the analytical goal desired and the reasonable level of privacy expected.

In this paper we elaborate on the above ideas and instantiate the privacy-by-design paradigm, introduced by Anne Cavoukian [19], in the 1990s, to the designing of big data analytical services. First, we discuss the privacy-by-design principle highlighting how it has been embraced by United States and Europe. Then, we introduce our idea of privacy-by-design in big data analytics domain and show how inscribing privacy 'by design' in four different specific scenarios assuring a good balance between privacy protection and quality of data analysis. To this end, we review a method for a privacy-aware publication of movement data enabling clustering analysis useful for understanding human mobility behavior in specific urban areas [20], a method for a privacy-aware outsourcing of the pattern mining task [21], and a method for a privacy-aware distributed mobility data analytics [22], enabling any company without suitable resources to take advantage from data mining technologies. Finally, we analyze the privacy issues of the socio-meter of urban population presented in [23] and propose a privacy-by-design schema that allows a privacy-aware estimation of the proportion of city users that fall into three categories: residents, commuters, visitors. Especially in this last example, we can see how sometimes it is sufficient to use a bit of smartness in order to have good quality results without compromising individual privacy.

The remaining of the paper is organized as following. In Section 2 we discuss the privacy-by-design paradigm and its articulation in data analytics. Section 3 and Section 4 discuss the application of the privacy-by-design principle in the case of publication of personal mobility trajectories and outsourcing of mining tasks, respectively. In Section 5 we show a possible distributed scenario for privacy preserving mobility analytics, while in Section 6 we present a study of privacy issues of a socio-meter of urban population and propose a schema for guaranteeing user privacy protection. Lastly, Section 7 concludes the paper.

2 Privacy-by-design

Privacy-by-design is a paradigm developed by Ontario's Information and Privacy Commissioner, Dr. Ann Cavoukian, in the 1990s, to address the emerging and growing threats to online privacy. The main idea is to inscribe the privacy protection into the design of information technologies from the very start. This paradigm represents a significant innovation with respect to the traditional approaches of privacy protection because it requires a significant shift from a reactive model to proactive one. In other words, the idea is preventing privacy issues instead of remedying to them.

Given the ever growing diffusion and availability of big data and given the great impact of the big data analytics on both human privacy risks and the possibility of understanding important phenomena many companies are realizing the necessity to consider privacy at every stage of their business and thus, to integrate privacy requirements 'by design' into their business model. Unfortunately, in many contexts it is not completely clear which are the methodologies for incorporating privacy-by-design.

2.1 Privacy-by-design in law

The privacy-by-design model has been embraced in Europe and in the United States.

In 2010, at the annual conference of 'Data Protection and Privacy Commissioners' the International Privacy Commissioners and Data Protection Authorities approved a resolution recognizing privacy-by-design as an *essential component of fundamental privacy protection* [24] and encourages the adoption of this principle as part of an organization's default mode of operation.

In 2009, the EU Article 29 Data Protection Working Party and the Working Party on Police and Justice released a joint Opinion, recommending the incorporation of the principles of privacy-by-design into a new EU privacy framework [25]. In March 2010, the European Data Protection Supervisor suggested to 'include unequivocally and explicitly the principle of privacy-by-design into the existing data protection regulatory framework' [26]. This recommendation was taken into consideration in the recent revision of the Data Protection Directive (95/46/EC) currently under discussion at EC. The European Union Data Protection Directive has always included provisions requiring data controllers to implement *technical and organizational measures* in the design and operation of ICT; but this has proven insufficient. Therefore, in the comprehensive reform of the data protection rules proposed on January 25, 2012, the new data protection legal framework introduces, with respect to the Directive 95/46/EC, the reference to *data protection by design and by default* (Article 23 of the Proposal for a Regulation). This article compels the controller to '*implement appropriate technical and organizational measures and procedures in such a way that the processing will meet the requirements of this Regulation and ensure the protection of the rights of the data subject*' and to '*implement mechanisms for ensuring that, by default, only those personal data are processed which are necessary for each specific purpose of the processing…*'.

Privacy-by-design has been embraced also in the United States. In the last years the U.S. Federal Trade Commission hosted a series of public roundtable discussions on privacy issues in the digital age and in a recent staff report [27] it describes a proposed framework with three main recommendations: *privacy-by-design, simplified consumer choice*, and *increased transparency of data practices*. Moreover, some pieces of legislation have also been proposed and introduced which include the principles of privacy-by-design, including:

(a) in April 2011, Senators John Kerry (D-MA) and John McCain (R-AZ) proposed their legislation entitled 'Commercial Privacy Bill of Rights Act of 2011' that, if passed, would require companies that collect, use, store or transfer consumer information to implement a version of privacy-by-design when developing products; (b) the Franken/Blumenthal Location Privacy Protection Act, introduced in 2012, that regulates the transmission and sharing of user location data in USA; and (b) the Wyden/Chaffetz Geolocation and Privacy Surveillance, introduced in 2011, that attempted to limit government surveillance using geolocation information such as signals from mobile phones and GPS devices.

2.2 Privacy-by-design in big data analytics and social mining

As stated above, in many contexts it is not clear what means applying the privacy-by-design principle and which is the best way to apply it for obtaining the desired result. In this section, we discuss the articulation of the general 'by design' principle in the big data analytics domain.

Our main idea is to inscribe privacy protection into any analytical process by design, so that the analysis incorporates the relevant privacy requirements from the very start, evoking the concept of privacy-by-design discussed above.

The articulation of the general 'by design' principle in the big data analytics domain is that higher protection and quality can be better achieved in a goal-oriented approach. In such an approach, the data analytical process is designed with assumptions about:

(a) the sensitive personal data subject of the analysis;
(b) the attack model, i.e., the knowledge and purpose of adversary that has an interest in discovering the sensitive data of certain individuals;
(c) the category of analytical queries that are to be answered with the data.

These assumptions are fundamental for the design of a privacy-aware technology. First of all, the techniques for privacy preservation strongly depend on the nature of the data to be protected. For example, methods suitable for social networking data could not be appropriate for trajectory data.

Second, a valid framework has to define the attack model, that could be an honest-but-curious adversary model or a malicious adversary model, and an adequate countermeasure. The two models require different actions due to their characteristics. The first one executes protocols correctly but tries to learn as much as possible. For example, by reading off-line the standard output of the algorithm he can try to deduce information on the other party. This is different from the malicious adversary who since could also deviate arbitrarily from the protocol is harder to be countered. Typically an attack is based on a specific adversary's background knowledge and different assumptions on the background knowledge entail different defense strategies. For example, an attacker could possess an approximated information about the mobility behavior of a person and use it to infer all his movements. In other cases, the adversary could shadow a person and discover some specific places visited by him obtaining an exact information. It is clear that a defense strategy designed for counter attacks with approximate knowledge could be too weak in case of detailed knowledge and vice versa.

Finally, a privacy-aware strategy should find an acceptable trade-off between data privacy and data utility. To this end, it is fundamental to consider the category of analytical queries to be answered for understanding which data properties is necessary to preserve. As an example, the design of a defense strategy for movement data should consider that this data could be used for analyzing collective mobility behavior in a urban area.

Under the above assumptions, we claim that it is conceivable to design a privacy-aware analytical process that can:

1. transform the data into an anonymous version with a quantifiable privacy guarantee - i.e., the probability that the malicious attack fails;

2. guarantee that a category of analytical queries can be answered correctly, within a quantifiable approximation that specifies the data utility, using the transformed data instead of the original ones.

The trade-off between privacy protection and data quality must be the main goal in the design of a privacy-aware technology for big data analytics. If in the designing of a such framework only one of these two aspects is taken into consideration, then the consequence is that either we assure high levels of privacy but the data cannot be used for analytical scopes, or we assure a very good quality of data by putting at risk the individual privacy protection of people in the data. Note that, in big data analytics and social mining typically one is interested into extract collective knowledge and this could not involve the use of personally identifiable information. However, when it does, the *data minimization* principle should be taken into account, since it allows managing data privacy risks, by effectively eliminating risk at the earliest stage of the information life cycle. This principle requires that in the design of big data analytical frameworks we should consider that we need no collection of personally identifiable information, unless a specific purpose is defined. The above privacy-by-design methodology (Point c) can help to understand which is the minimal information that enables a good analysis and protection. As we can see in the scenario presented in Section 6, we are able to find the minimal information for mining data with perfect quality and, we show how the level of data aggregation useful for the analysis already provides very low privacy risks.

In the following, we show how we apply the privacy-by-design paradigm for the design of four analytical frameworks: one for the publication of trajectory data; one for the outsourcing of data mining tasks; one for computing aggregation of movement data in a distributed fashion and one for the quantification of user profiles in GSM data. In the four scenarios we first analyze the privacy issues related to this kind of data, second, we identify the attack model and third, we provide a method for assuring data privacy taking into consideration the data analysis to be maintained valid. However, these are not the unique privacy-preserving frameworks adopting the privacy-by-design principle, many approaches proposed in the literature can be seen as instances of this promising paradigm (see [14–18]).

3 Privacy-by-design in mobility data publishing

In this section, we discuss a framework that offers an instance of the privacy by design paradigm in the case of personal mobility trajectories (obtained from GPS devices or cell phones) [20]. It is suitable for the privacy-aware publication of movement data enabling clustering analysis useful for the understanding of human mobility behavior in specific urban areas. The released trajectories are make anonymous by a suitable process that realizes a generalized version of the original trajectories.

The framework is based on a data-driven spatial generalization of the dataset of trajectories. The results obtained with the application of this framework show how trajectories can be anonymized to a high level of protection against re-identification while preserving the possibility of mining clusters of trajectories, which enables novel powerful analytic services for info-mobility or location-based services. We highlight that the mobility data published after the privacy transformation strategy, described in the following, is suitable for collective data analyses useful for extracting knowledge describing the collective mobility behavior of a population. Clearly, in cases where for providing a service it is necessary to identify specific, personal trajectories related to a specific user, this framework is not adequate. This because in that context one of the most important aspects is to maintain clear and well-defined the information at *individual* level, which is what we want to obfuscate with our transformation. In other words, the goal here is to *enable collective analytical tool while protecting the individual privacy*.

3.1 State-of-the-art on privacy-preserving mobility data publishing

There have been some works on privacy-preserving publishing of spatio-temporal moving points by using the generalization/suppression techniques. The mostly widely used privacy model of these works is adapted from what so called k-anonymity [28, 29], which requires that an individual should not be identifiable from a group of size smaller than k based on their quasi-identifies (QIDs), i.e., a set of attributes that can be used to uniquely identify the individuals. [14] proposes the (k, δ)-anonymity model that exploits the inherent uncertainty of the moving object's whereabouts, where δ represents possible location imprecision. Terrovitis and Mamoulis [30] assume that different adversaries own different, disjoint parts of the trajectories. Their anonymization technique is based on *suppression* of the dangerous observations from each trajectory. Yarovoy et al. [31] consider timestamps as the quasi-identifiers, and define a method based on *k-anonymity* to defend against an attack called *attack graphs*. Nergiz et al. [32] provide privacy protection by: (1) first enforcing k-anonymity, i.e. all released information refers to at least k users/trajectories, (2) randomly reconstructing a representation of the original dataset from the anonymization. Recently, [15] propose a anonymization technique based on microaggregation and perturbation. The advantage of this approach is to obtain anonymous data preserving real locations in the data and t this goal the transformation strategy uses swapping of locations.

All the above anonymization approaches are based on randomization techniques, space translations or swapping of points, and the suppression of various portions of a trajectory. To the best of our knowledge only [20] uses data-driven spatial generalization to achieve anonymity for trajectory datasets; the only work applying spatial generalization is [31], but it uses a fixed grid hierarchy to discretize the spatial dimension. In contrast, the novelty of our approach lies in finding a suitable tessellation of the geographical area into subareas dependent on the input trajectory dataset and in taking into consideration from the start also the analytical properties to be preserved in the data for guaranteeing good performance in terms of clustering analysis.

3.2 Attack and privacy model

In this framework the *linkage attack model* is considered, i.e., the ability to link the published data to external information, which enables some respondents associated with the data to be re-identified. In relational data, linking is made possible by *quasi-identifiers*, i.e., attributes that, in combination, can uniquely identify individuals, such as birth date and gender [28]. The remaining attributes represent the private respondent's information, that may be violated by the linkage attack. In privacy-preserving data publishing techniques, such as k-anonymity, the goal is precisely to find countermeasures to this attack, and to release person-specific data in such a way that the ability to link to other information using the quasi-identifier(s) is limited. In the case of spatio-temporal data, where each record is a temporal sequence of locations visited by a specific person, the above dichotomy of attributes into quasi-identifiers (QI) and private information (PI) does not hold any longer: here, a (sub)trajectory can play both the role of QI and the role of PI. To see this point, consider the attacker may know a sequence of places visited by some specific person P: e.g., by shadowing P for some time, the attacker may learn that P was in the shopping mall, then in the park, and then at the train station. The attacker could employ such knowledge to retrieve the complete trajectory of P in the released dataset: this attempt would succeed, provided that the attacker knows that P's trajectory is actually present in the dataset, if the known trajectory is compatible with (i.e., is a sub-trajectory of) just one trajectory in the dataset. In this example of a linkage attack in the movement data domain, the sub-trajectory known by the attacker serves as QI, while the entire trajectory is the PI that is disclosed after the re-identification of the respondent. Clearly, as the example suggests, it is rather difficult to distinguish QI and PI: in principle, any specific location can be the theater of a shadowing action by a spy, and therefore any possible sequence of locations can be used as a QI, i.e., as a means for re-identification. As a consequence of this discussion, it is reasonable to consider the radical assumption that any (sub)trajectory that can be linked to a small number of individuals is a potentially dangerous QI and a potentially sensitive PI. Therefore, in the *trajectory linkage attack*, the malicious party M knows a sub-trajectory of a respondent R (e.g., a sequence of locations where R has been spied on by M) and M would like to identify in the data the whole trajectory belonging to R, i.e., learn all places visited by R.

3.3 Privacy-preserving technique

How is it possible to guarantee that the probability of success of the above attack is very low while preserving the utility of the data for meaningful analyses? Consider the source trajectories represented in Figure 1(a), obtained from a massive dataset of GPS traces (17,000 private vehicles tracked in the city of Milan, Italy, during a week).

Each trajectory is a de-identified sequence of time-stamped locations, visited by one of the tracked vehicles. Albeit de-identified, each trajectory is essentially unique - very rarely two different trajectories are exactly the same given the extremely fine spatio-temporal resolution involved. As a consequence, the chances of success for the trajectory linkage

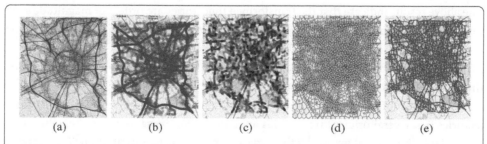

(a)   (b)   (c)   (d)   (e)

Figure 1 Trajectory Generalization process. (a) Original trajectories from Milan GPS dataset; (b) simplification of trajectory points by considering only relevant events (start, end, turns); (c) relevant points are clustered by spatial proximity to reveal zones with high frequency of movement events; (d) from the centroids of each cluster it is derived a voronoi tessellation of the territory; (e) original trajectories are generalized as sequence of traversed cells of the previous tessellation.

attack are not low. If the attacker M knows a sufficiently long sub-sequence S of locations visited by the respondent R, it is possible that only a few trajectories in the dataset match with S, possibly just one. Indeed, publishing raw trajectory data such as those depicted in Figure 1(a) is an unsafe practice, which runs a high risk of violating the private sphere of the tracked drivers (e.g., guessing the home place and the work place of most respondents is very easy). Now, assume that one wants to discover the trajectory clusters emerging from the data through data mining, i.e., the groups of trajectories sharing common mobility behavior, such as the commuters following similar routes in their home-work and work-home trips. An privacy transformation of the trajectories consists of the following steps:

1. characteristic points are extracted from the original trajectories: starting points, ending points, points of significant turn, points of significant stop (Figure 1(b));
2. characteristic points are clustered into small groups by spatial proximity (Figure 1(c));
3. the central points of the groups are used to partition the space by means of Voronoi tessellation (Figure 1(d));
4. each original trajectory is transformed into the sequence of Voronoi cells that it crosses (Figure 1(e)).

As a result of this data-driven transformation, where trajectories are generalized from sequences of points to sequences of cells, the re-identification probability already drops significantly. Further techniques can be adopted to lower it even more, obtaining a safe theoretical upper bound for the worst case (i.e., the maximal probability that the linkage attack succeeds), and an extremely low average probability. A possible technique is to ensure that for any sub-trajectory used by the attacker, the re-identification probability is always controlled below a given threshold $\frac{1}{k}$; in other words, ensuring the k-anonymity property in the released dataset. Here, the notion of k-anonymity proposed is based on the definition of *k-harmful trajectory*, i.e., a trajectory occurring in the database with a frequency less than k. Therefore, a trajectory database D^* is considered a k-anonymous version of a database D if: each k-harmful trajectory in D appears at least k times in D^* or if it does not appear in D^* anymore. To achieve this k-anonymous database, the generalized trajectories, obtained after the data-driven transformation, are transformed in such a way that all the k-harmful sub-trajectories in D are not k-harmful in D^*. In the example in Figure 1(a), the probability of success is theoretically bounded by $\frac{1}{20}$ (i.e., 20-anonymity is achieved), but the real upper bound for 95% of attacks is below 10^{-3}.

3.4 Analytics quality

The above results indicate that the transformed trajectories are orders of magnitude safer than the original data in a measurable sense: *but are they still useful to achieve the desired result, i.e., discovering trajectory clusters?*

Figure 2(top) and Figure 2(down) illustrate the most relevant clusters found by mining the original trajectories and the anonymized trajectories, respectively.

A direct effect of the anonymization process is an increase in the concentration of trajectories (i.e. several original trajectories are bundled on the same route); the clustering method will thus be influenced by the variation in the density distribution. The increase in the concentration of trajectories is mainly caused by the reduction of noisy data. In fact, the anonymization process tends to make each trajectory similar to the neighboring ones. This means that the original trajectories, initially classified as noise, can now be 'promoted' as members of a cluster. This phenomenon may produce an enlarged version of

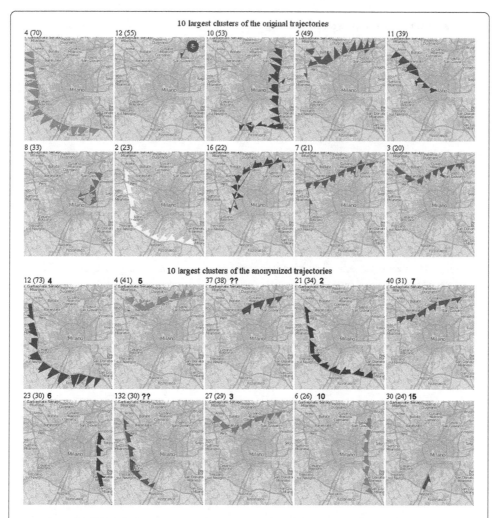

Figure 2 Comparison of the 10 largest clusters of the original trajectories (top) and of the anonymized trajectories (down). Each map summaries the trajectories within a single cluster by directed arrows with thickness proportional to flow. Bottom maps have a reference to the cluster id (in bold) of original trajectories with a similar shape.

the original clusters. To evaluate the clustering preservation quantitively the F-measure is adopted. The F-measure is usually adopted to express the combined values of precision and recall and is defined as the harmonic mean of the two measures. Here, the recall measures how the cohesion of a cluster is preserved: it is 1 if the whole original cluster is mapped into a single anonymized cluster, it tends to zero if the original elements are scattered among several anonymized clusters. The precision measures how the singularity of a cluster is mapped into the anonymized version: if the anonymized cluster contains only elements corresponding to the original cluster its value is 1, otherwise the value tends to zero if there are other elements corresponding to other clusters. The contamination of an anonymized cluster may depend on two factors: (i) there are elements corresponding to other original clusters or (ii) there are elements that were formerly noise and have been promoted to members of an anonymized cluster.

The immediate visual perception that the resulting clusters are very similar in the two cases in Figures 2(top) and 2(down) is also confirmed by various cluster comparisons by Precision, Recall and F-measure, re-defined for clustering comparison (Figure 3). Here,

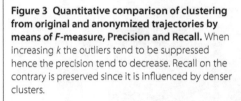

Figure 3 Quantitative comparison of clustering from original and anonymized trajectories by means of *F*-measure, Precision and Recall. When increasing *k* the outliers tend to be suppressed hence the precision tend to decrease. Recall on the contrary is preserved since it is influenced by denser clusters.

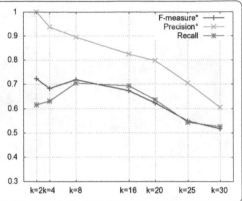

precision measures the percentage of objects that are preserved within the same transformed cluster; *recall* measures the percentage of objects of a transformed cluster that were into the same original cluster; *F*-measure is the harmonic mean of the previous measures.

The conclusion is that in the illustrated process the desired quality of the analytical results can be achieved in a privacy-preserving setting with concrete formal safeguards and the protection w.r.t. the linkage attack can be measured.

4 Privacy-by-design in data mining outsourcing

In this section, we discuss an instance of the privacy by design paradigm, in the case of outsourcing of the pattern mining task [21]; in particular, the results show how a company can outsource the transaction data to a third party and obtain a data mining service in a privacy-preserving manner.

The particular problem of *outsourcing mining tasks within a privacy-preserving framework* is very interesting and is acquiring novel relevance with the advent of cloud computing and its model for IT services based on the Internet and big data centers. Business intelligence and knowledge discovery services, such as advanced analytics based on data mining technologies, are expected to be among the services amenable to be externalized on the cloud, due to their data intensive nature, as well as the complexity of data mining algorithms.

However, the key business analysis functions are unlikely to be outsourced, as they represent a strategic asset of a company: what is instead appealing for a company is to rely on external expertise and infrastructure for the data mining task, i.e., how to compute the analytical results and models which are required by the business analysts for understanding the business phenomena under observation. As an example, the operational transactional data from various stores of a supermarket chain can be shipped to a third party which provides mining services. The supermarket management need not employ an in-house team of data mining experts. Besides, they can cut down their local data management requirements because periodically data is shipped to the service provider who is in charge of maintaining it and conducting mining on it in response to requests from business analysts of the supermarket chain.

Although it is advantageous to achieve sophisticated analysis there exist several serious privacy issues of the data-mining-as-a-service paradigm. One of the main issues is that the server has access to valuable data of the owner and may learn sensitive information from it.

A key distinction between this problem and the privacy-preserving data mining and data publishing problems is that, in this setting, not only the underlying data but also the mined results (the strategic information) are not intended for sharing and must remain private. In particular, when the third party possesses background knowledge and conducts attacks on that basis, it should not be able to learn new knowledge with a probability above a given threshold.

The frameworks devised to protect privacy in this setting have also to preserve the data utility. *What does data utility mean in this specific context?* In general, a framework for protecting the corporate privacy in data mining outsourcing must guarantee: (1) to the data owner the possibility to query its data in outsourcing (2) to the server provider to answer the queries of the data owner with an encrypted result that does not allow to infer any knowledge (3) to the data owner to recover the query results within a quantifiable approximation. The approximation of the point (3) specifies the data utility guaranteed by the privacy-preserving framework.

4.1 State-of-the-art on privacy-preserving data mining outsourcing

There have been some works on privacy-preserving data mining outsourcing. Note that, the application of a simple substitution ciphers to the items of the original database is not enough to protect privacy in this setting. Indeed, an intruder could use information about the item frequency for inferring the real identity of the items and as a consequence for breaking the whole database and the possible knowledge represented into it.

The approach in [33] is based on outsourcing a randomized dataset that is transformed by means of Bloom filters: compared with our proposal, the main weakness of this approach is that it only supports an approximate reconstruction of the mined frequent itemsets by the data owner, while our encryption/decryption method supports reconstruction of the *exact* supports.

The works that are most related to ours are [18] and [34]. They assume that the adversary possesses prior knowledge of the frequency of items or item sets, which can be used to try to re-identify the encrypted items. Wong et al. [18] consider an attack model where the attacker knows the frequency of $\alpha\%$ of frequent itemsets to within $\pm\beta\%$, while our attack model focuses on single items with the assumption that the attacker knows the exact frequency of every single item, i.e., ours is a $(100\%, 0\%)$ attack model, but confined to items. Authors in [34] assume the attacker knows exact frequency of single items, similarly to us. Both [18] and [34] use similar privacy model as ours, which requires that each real item must have the same frequency count as $k - 1$ other items in the outsourced dataset. The major issue left open by [18] is a formal protection result: their privacy analysis is entirely conducted empirically on various synthetic datasets. Tai et al. [34] show that their outsourced data set satisfies k-support anonymity, but only explores set based attack empirically. Unfortunately, both works have potential privacy flaws: Molloy et al. [35] show how privacy can be breached in the framework of [18]. We have discuss the details of the flaws in the framework of [34] in [21].

4.2 Attack and privacy model

In the proposed framework, in order to achieve a strong data protection, the assumption is that an attacker wants to acquire information on the sale data and the mined patterns by using rich background information. In particular, the attacker knows with precision the set of items in the original transaction database and their popularity, i.e., how many times each individual item is sold. This information can be obtained from a competing company or from published reports.

More formally, let D be the original transaction database that the owner has and D^* its private version. The server or an intruder, who gains access to it, may possess some background knowledge using which they can conduct attacks on the encrypted database D^*. The attacker knows exactly the set of (plain) items $\mathcal{I}$ in the original transaction database D and their true supports in D. The service provider (who can be an attacker) can use his background knowledge to make inferences on the encrypted transactions D^*. The data owner (i.e., the corporate) considers the true identity of every cipher item, every cipher transaction, and every cipher frequent pattern as the intellectual property which should be protected. Therefore, the following attacks are considered:

- *Item-based attack*: $\forall$ cipher item $e \in \mathcal{E}$, the attacker constructs a set of candidate plain items $\text{Cand}(e) \subset \mathcal{I}$. The probability that the cipher item e can be broken $\text{prob}(e) = 1/|\text{Cand}(e)|$.
- *Set-based attack*: Given a cipher itemset E, the attacker constructs a set of candidate plain itemsets $\text{Cand}(E)$, where $\forall X \in \text{Cand}(E)$, $X \subset \mathcal{I}$, and $|X| = |E|$. The probability that the cipher itemset E can be broken $\text{prob}(E) = 1/|\text{Cand}(E)|$.

We refer to $\text{prob}(e)$ and $\text{prob}(E)$ as *crack probabilities*. From the point of view of the owner, minimizing the probabilities of crack is desirable. Clearly, $\text{Cand}(e)$ and $\text{Cand}(E)$ should be as large as possible; in particular, $\text{Cand}(e)$ should be the whole set of plaintext items. This can be achieved by bringing each cipher item to the same level of support, e.g., to the support of the most frequent item in D. This option would lead to a dramatic explosion of the frequent patterns making pattern mining at the server side computationally prohibitive. [21] proposes of relaxing the equal-support constraint introducing item k-anonymity as a compromise.

4.3 Privacy-preserving technique

How to counter the above attacks while assuring for the client the ability of obtaining the correct collection of frequent patterns? A possible solution is applying an encryption scheme that transforms the original database by the following steps: (I) replacing each item by a 1-1 substitution function; and (II) adding fake transactions to the database in such a way that each item (itemset) becomes indistinguishable with at least $k-1$ other items (itemsets). On the basis of this simple idea, this framework guarantees that not only individual items, but also any group of items has the property of being indistinguishable from at least k other groups in the worst case, and actually many more in the average case. This protection implies that the attacker has a very limited probability of guessing the actual items contained either in the sale data or in the mining results. On the contrary, the data owner can efficiently decrypt correct mining results, returned by the third party, with limited computational resources. Indeed, the framework provides a very efficient decryption schema that uses very negligibly small information representing in a compact way the information about the fake transactions added during the encryption phase. This research shows interesting results obtained applying this model over large-scale, real-life transaction databases donated by a large supermarket chain in Europe. The architecture behind the proposed model is illustrated in Figure 4. The client/owner encrypts its transaction database (TDB)

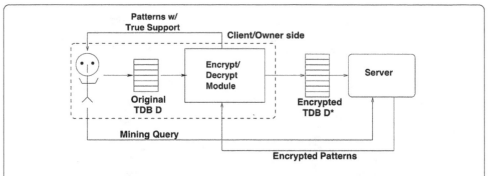

Figure 4 Architecture of Mining-as-Service Paradigm showing that the client before sending data to the server encrypts it and the server answers the mining queries with encrypted patterns that the client can decrypt before their use.

using an encrypt/decrypt module, which can be essentially treated as a 'black box' from its perspective. This module is responsible for transforming the TDB D into an encrypted database D^*. The server conducts data mining and sends the (encrypted) patterns to the owner. The encryption scheme has the property that the returned number of occurrences of the patterns are not true. The encrypt/decrypt module recovers the true identity of the returned patterns as well their true number of occurrences.

The strong theoretical results in [21] show a remarkable guarantee of protection against the attacks presented in Section 4.2, and the practicability and the effectiveness of the proposed schema. The application of this framework on real-world databases showed that the privacy protection is much better than the theoretical worst case. *Why?* The explanation is that the probability of crack generally decreases with the size of the itemset: $\frac{1}{k}$ is an upper bound that essentially applies only to individual items, not itemsets (under the hypothesis that the adopted grouping is robust).

4.4 Frequent pattern mining and privacy protection

The framework is applied to real-world data donated us by Coop, a cooperative of consumers that is today the largest supermarket chain in Italy. The data contain transactions occurring during four periods of time in a subset of Coop stores, creating in this way four different databases with varying number of transactions: from 100k to 400k transactions. In all the datasets the transactions involve 15,713 different products grouped into 366 marketing categories. Two distinct kind of databases are considered: (i) product-level (*Coop-Prod*) where items correspond to products, and (ii) category-level databases (*CoopCat*), where items are category of the products.

Crack probability. The analysis of the crack probability for transactions and patterns in both databases *CoopProd* and *CoopCat* highlighted that after the data transformation around 90% of the transactions can be broken with probability strictly less than $\frac{1}{k}$. For example, considering the encrypted version of *CoopProd* with 300K transactions, the experiments showed the following facts, even for small k. For instance, for $k = 10$, every transaction E has at least 10 plain itemset candidates, i.e., $\mathrm{prob}(E) \leq \frac{1}{10}$. Around 5% of transactions have exactly a crack probability $\frac{1}{10}$, while 95% have a probability strictly smaller than $\frac{1}{10}$. Around 90% have a probability strictly smaller than $\frac{1}{100}$.

Frequent pattern mining. The schema proposed, i.e., the *encryption* of the transactions and the *decryption* of the patterns enable the client to recover the true identity of the

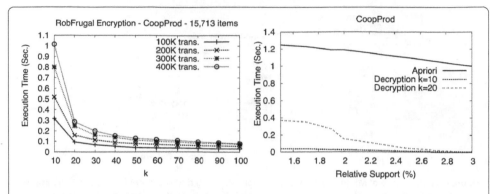

Figure 5 Encryption and Decryption Overhead. (Left) Encryption Overhead by varying the *k* value and the number of transactions; (Right) Comparison of Decryption Overhead and mining cost on the original data using Apriori by varying the minimum support threshold for the pattern extraction.

returned patterns as well their true number of occurrences. Therefore, for the client there is no quality loss for the set of the mined patterns.

An important aspect in the data mining outsourcing is the efficiency of the encryption/decryption schema because one of the motivation of the data mining outsourcing is the lack of computational resources for mining of some companies. In Figure 5(left) we can see that, when there are multiple mining queries, which is always the case for the outsourcing system, the encryption overhead of the proposed scheme is negligible compared with the cost of mining. Figure 5(right) shows that the decryption time is about one order of magnitude smaller than the mining time; for higher support threshold, the gap increases to about two orders of magnitude. The situation is similar in CoopCat. The results also show that the encryption time is always small; it is under 1 second for the biggest *Coop-Prod*, and below 0.8 second for the biggest *CoopCat*. Moreover, it is always less than the time of a single mining query, which is at least 1 second by Apriori (Figure 5(right)).

5 Privacy-by-design in distributed analytical systems

The previous Section 3 and Section 4 how we can apply the privacy-by-design methodology for guaranteeing individual privacy in a setting where we have a central trusted aggregation center that collects data and before releasing it can apply a privacy transformation strategy to enable collective analyses in a privacy-aware fashion.

However, privacy-by-design paradigm can also be applied with success to distributed analytical systems where we have a untrusted central station that collects some aggregate statistics computed by each individual node that observes a stream of data. In this section we discuss an instance of this case [22]; in particular, we show as the privacy-by-design methodology can help in the design of a privacy-aware distributed analytical processing framework for the aggregation of movement data. We consider the data collector nodes as on-board location devices in vehicles that continuously trace the positions of vehicles and periodically send statistical information about their movements to a central station. The central station, which we call *coordinator*, will store the received statistical information and compute a summary of the traffic conditions of the whole territory, based on the information collected from data collectors.

We show how privacy can be obtained before data leaves users, ensuring the utility of some data analysis performed at collective level, also after the transformation. This example brings evidence to the fact that the privacy-by-design model has the potential of delivering high data protection combined with high quality even in massively distributed techno-social systems. As discussed in Section 3, the aim of this framework is to provide both *individual* privacy protection by the differential privacy model and acceptable *collective* data utility.

5.1 State-of-the-art on privacy-preserving distributed data analytics

A privacy model particularly suitable for guaranteeing individual privacy while answering to aggregate queries is *differential privacy* [36]. Recently, much attention has been paid to use differential privacy for distributed private data analysis. In this setting n parties, each holding some sensitive data, wish to compute some aggregate statistics over all parties' data with or without a centralized coordinator. [37, 38] prove that when computing the sum of all parties' inputs without a central coordinator, any differentially-private multi-party protocol with a small number of rounds and small number of messages must have large error. Rastogi et al. [39] and Chan et al. [40] consider the problem of privately aggregating sums over multiple time periods. Both of them consider malicious coordinator and use both encryption and differential privacy for the design of privacy-preserving data aggregation methods. Compared with their work, we focus on semi-honest coordinator, with the aim of designing privacy-preserving techniques by adding meaningful noises to improve data utility. Furthermore, both [39, 40] consider aggregate-sum queries as the main utility function, while we consider network flow based analysis for the collected data. Different utility models lead to different design of privacy-preserving techniques. We agree that our method can be further enforced to against the malicious coordinator by applying the encryption methods in [39, 40].

5.2 Attack and privacy model

As in the case analyzed in Section 3, we consider as sensitive information any data from which the typical mobility behavior of a user may be inferred. This information is considered sensitive for two main reasons: (1) typical movements can be used to identify the drivers who drive specific vehicles even when a simple de-identification of the individual in the system is applied; and (2) the places visited by a driver could identify peculiar sensitive areas such as clinics, hospitals and routine locations such as the user's home and workplace.

The assumption is that each node in the system is honest; in other words attacks at the node level are not considered. Instead, potential attacks are from any intruder between the node and the coordinator (i.e., attacks during the communications), and from any intruder at coordinator site, so this privacy preserving technique has to guarantee privacy even against a malicious behavior of the coordinator. For example, the coordinator may be able to obtain real mobility statistic information from other sources, such as from public datasets on the web, or through personal knowledge about a specific participant, like in the previously (and diffusely) discussed linking attack.

The solution proposed in [22] is based on *Differential Privacy*, a recent model of randomization introduced in [41] by Dwork. The general idea of this paradigm is that the privacy risks should not increase for a respondent as a result of occurring in a statistical database; differential privacy ensures, in fact, that the ability of an adversary to inflict harm should be essentially the same, independently of whether any individual opts in to, or opts out of, the dataset. This privacy model is called ε-differential privacy, due to the level of privacy guaranteed ε. Note that when ε tends to 1 very little perturbation is introduced and this yields a low privacy protection; on the contrary, better privacy guarantees are obtained when ε tends to zero. Differential privacy assures a record owner that any privacy breach will not be a result of participating in the database since anything, or almost nothing, that is learnable from the database with his record is also learnable from the one without his data. Moreover, in [41] is formally proved that ε-differential privacy can provide a guarantee against adversaries with arbitrary background knowledge, thus, in this case we do not need to define any explicit background knowledge for attackers.

Here, we do not provide the formal definition of this paradigm, but we only point out that the mechanism of differential privacy works by adding appropriately chosen random noise (from a specific distribution) to the true answer, then returning the perturbed answer. A little variant of this model is the (ε, δ)-differential privacy, where the noise is bounded at the cost of introducing a privacy loss. A key notion used by differential privacy mechanisms is the *sensitivity* of a query, that provides a way to set the noise distribution in order to calibrate the noise magnitude on the basis of the type of query. The sensitivity measures the maximum distance between the same query executed on two close datasets, i.e., datasets differing on one single element (either a user or a event). As an example, consider a count query on a medical dataset, which returns the number of patients having a particular disease. The result of the query performed on two close datasets, i.e., differing exactly on one patient, can change at most by 1; thus, in this case (or, more generally, in count query cases), the sensitivity is 1.

The questions are: *How can we hide the event that the user moved from a location* a *to a location* b *in a time interval τ? And how can we hide the real count of moves in that time window?* In other words, *How can we enable collective movement data aggregation for mobility analysis while guaranteeing individual privacy protection?* The solution that we report is based on (ε, δ)-differential privacy, and provides a good balance between privacy and data utility.

5.3 Privacy-preserving technique

First of all, each participant must share a common partition of the examined territory; for this purpose, it is possible to use an existing division of the territory (e.g., census sectors, road segments, etc.) or to determine a data-driven partition as the Voronoi tessellation introduced in Section 3.3. Once the partition is shared, each trajectory is generalized as a sequence of crossed areas (i.e., a sequence of movements). For convenience's sake, this information is mapped onto a *frequency vector*, linked to the partition. Unfortunately, releasing frequency of moves instead of raw trajectory data to the coordinator is not privacy-preserving, as the intruder may still infer the sensitive typical movement information of the driver. As an example, the attacker could learn the driver's most frequent move; this information can be very sensitive because such move usually corresponds to a user's transportation between home and workplace. Thus, the proposed solution relies on the differential privacy mechanism, using a Laplace distribution [36]. At the end of the predefined time interval τ, before sending the frequency vector to the coordinator, for each element in the vector the node extracts the noise from the Laplace distribution and adds it to the original value in that position of the vector. At the end of this step the node V_j transformed its frequency vector f_{V_j} into its private version $\tilde{f}_{V_j}$. This ensures the respect of the ε-differential privacy. This simple general strategy has some drawbacks:

first, it could lead to large amount of noise that, although with small probability, can be arbitrarily large; second, adding noise drawn from the Laplace distribution could generate negative frequency counts of moves, which does not make sense in mobility scenarios. To fix these two problems, it is possible to bound the noise drawn from the Laplace distribution, reducing to an (ε, δ) differential privacy schema. In particular, for each value x of the vector f_{V_j}, it is possible to draw the noise bounding it in the interval $[-x, x]$. In other words, for any original frequency $f_{V_j}[i] = x$, its perturbed version after adding noise should be in the interval $[0, 2x]$. This approach satisfies (ε, δ)-differential privacy, where δ measures the privacy loss. Note that, since in a distributed environment a crucial problem is the overhead of communications, it is possible to reduce the amount of transmitted information, i.e., the size of frequency vectors. In [22], a possible solution of this problem is reported, but given that this is beyond the purpose of the current paper, we omit this kind of discussion.

5.4 Analytical quality

So far we presented the formal guarantees to individual privacy preservation, but we have to show yet if the individually transformed values are still useful once they are collected and aggregated by the coordinator, i.e., if they are still suitable at collective level for analysis. In the proposed framework, the coordinator collects the perturbed frequency vectors from all the vehicles in the time interval τ and sums them movement by movement. This allows obtaining the resulting global frequency vector, which represents the flow values for each link of the spatial tessellation. Since the privacy transformation operates on the entries of the frequency vectors, and hence on the flows, we present the comparison (before and after the transformation) of two measures: (1) the *Flow per Link*, i.e. the directed volume of traffic between two adjacent zones; (2) the *Flow per Zone*, i.e. the sum of the incoming and outgoing flows in a zone. The following results refer to the application of this technique on a large dataset of GPS vehicles traces, collected in a period from 1st May to 31st May 2011, in the geographical areas around Pisa, in central Italy. It counts for around 4,200 vehicles, generating around 15,700 trips. The τ interval is one day, so the global frequency vector represents the sum all the trajectories crossing any link, at the end of each day.

Figure 6 shows the resulting Complementary Cumulative Distribution Functions (CCDFs) of different privacy transformation varying ε from 0.9 to 0.01. Figure 6(left) shows the reconstructed flows per link: fixed a value of flow (x) we count the number of links (y) that have that flow. Figure 6(right) shows the distribution of sum of flows passing for each zone: given a flow value (x) it shows how many zones (y) present that total flow. From the distributions we can notice how the privacy transformation preserves very well the distribution of the original flows, even for more restrictive values of the parameter ε. Also considering several flows together, like those incident to a given zone (Figure 6(right)), the distributions are well preserved for all the privacy transformations. These results reveal how a method which *locally* perturbs values, at a *collective* level permits to obtain a very high utility.

Qualitatively, Figure 7 shows a visually comparison of results of the privacy transformation with the original ones. This is an example of two kind of visual analyses that can be performed using mobility data. Since the global complementary cumulative distribution functions are comparable, we can choose a very low epsilon ($\varepsilon = 0.01$) with the aim to

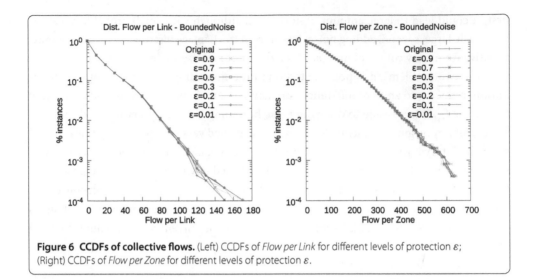

Figure 6 CCDFs of collective flows. (Left) CCDFs of *Flow per Link* for different levels of protection ε; (Right) CCDFs of *Flow per Zone* for different levels of protection ε.

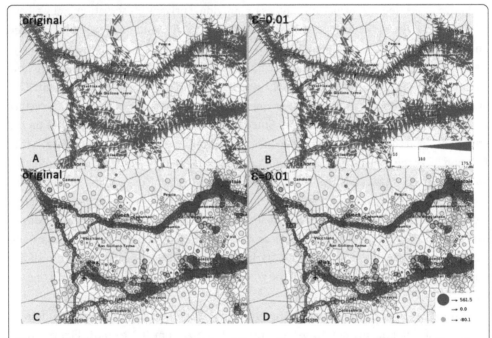

Figure 7 Visual comparison of *Flow per Link* and *Flow per Zone* measures: the resulting overview after the privacy transformation preserves relevant information and properties. Top: flows are rendered as arrows with width proportional to the flow between two regions. Bottom: flow in a region is represented as a circle whose radius is proportional to deviation from median volume in all zones.

emphasize the very good quality of mobility analysis that an analyst can obtain even if the data are transformed by using a very low ε value, i.e. obtaining a better privacy protection. In Figure 7(A) and (B) each flow is drawn with arrows with thickness proportional to the volume of trajectories observed on a link. From the figure it is evident how the relevant flows are preserved in the transformed global frequency vector, revealing the major highways and urban centers. Similarly, the *Flow per Zone* is also preserved, as it is shown in Figure 7(C) and (D), where the flow per each cell is rendered with a circle of radius proportional to the difference from the median value of each global frequency vector. The maps allow us to recognize the dense areas (red circles, above the median) separated by sparse

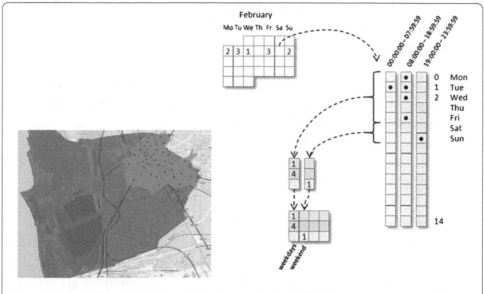

Figure 8 Methodology for GSM User Profile Construction. (Left) GSM Cell coverage in the area of Pisa; (Right) Schematic representation of reconstruction of the Temporal Profile for users in Pisa.

areas (blu circle below the median). The high density traffic zones follow the highways and the major city centers along their routes. The two comparisons proposed above give the intuition that, while the transformations protect individual sensitive information, the utility of data is preserved.

6 Privacy-by-design in user profiling in GSM data

In this section we study the privacy guarantees of the knowledge discovery process introduced in [23] and we show that it can be made in a privacy by design manner by applying some small change to the process that will not affect the final result of the analysis.

In [23] the authors present an analytical process for user profiling in GSM data; in other words, the proposed methodology identifies a partition of the users tracked by GSM phone calls into profiles like *resident*, *commuters* and *visitors* and quantifies the percentage of the different profiles.

The profiling methodology is based on an machine learning step using SOM [42] applied to spatio-temporal user profiles extracted from people call habits. In particular, the whole analytical process is composed of the following steps:

1. Select from the whole network the cells overlapping the area to which we are interested for the analysis (see Figure 8(left) as an example);

2. Build a time projection by two temporal operations (Figure 8(right)): (a) the aggregation of the days in weekdays and weekend slots; (b) the splitting of each slot in time intervals representing 3 interesting time windows during the day;

3. Construct for each user the Space Constrained Temporal Profile (SCT profile) [23] by using the CDR logs according to the space constraints (Point 1.) and the time projection (Point 2.). A SCT profile P is an aggregation of call statistics according to a given temporal discretization where only the calls performed in the cells, contained within the a certain area, are considered. In particular, each profile P is a matrix and each position P_{ij} contains the value v that corresponds to the number of days with at least one call from the user in the area of interest during the set of days j and the time

slot i. As an example, in Figure 8(right), $P_{2,1} = 4$ means that the user visited the area of interest 4 days during the weekdays of the first week and always in the time interval [08:00:00-18:59:59]. In the following we denote by $\mathcal{P}$ the set of SCT profiles extracted from CDR logs.

4. The set of SCT profiles, that are a concise representation of the users' behaviors measured by their calls, is then processed by using the SOM algorithm in order to extract the typical global profiles.

5. The SOM output is a set of nodes representing groups of users with similar temporal profiles; therefore, counting the instances in each group, it is possible to estimate the percentage of residents, commuters and visitors.

6.1 State-of-the-art on privacy in GSM data

Relatively, little work has addressed privacy issues in the publication and analysis of GSM data. In the literature, many works that treat GSM data state that in this context there is no privacy issue or at least the privacy problems are mitigated by the granularity of the cell phone. However, recently Golle and Partridge [43] showed that a fraction of the US working population can be uniquely identified by their *home* and *work* locations even when those locations are not known at a fine scale or granularity. Given that the locations most frequently visited by a mobile user often correspond to the home and work places, the risk in releasing locations traces of mobile phone users appears very high.

Privacy risks even in case of releasing of location information with not fine granularity are studied in [44]. In particular, authors look at the same problem of [43] but from a different perspective. They consider the 'top N' locations visited by each user instead of the simple home and work. The basic idea of this work is that more generally the number N of top preferential locations determines the power of an adversary and the safety of a user's privacy. Therefore, we can say that more top locations an adversary knows about a user, the higher is the probability to re-identify that user. The fewer top locations a user has, the safer they are in terms of privacy. [44] presents a study on 30 billion CDRs from a nationwide cellular service provider in the United States with location information for about 25 million mobile phone users on a period of three months. The study highlights important factors that can have a relevant impact on the anonymity. Examples are the value of N in finding the top N locations, the granularity level of the released locations, the fact that the top locations are sorted or not, the availability of additional social information about users, and geographical regions. The outcomes of this study is that the publication of anonymized location data in its original format, i.e. at the sector level or cell level, put at risk the user privacy because a significant fraction of users can be re-identified from the anonymized data. Moreover, it was shown that different geographical areas have different levels of privacy risks, and at a different granularity level this risk may be higher or lower than other areas. When the spatial granularity level of the cell data is combined with time information and a unique handset identifier, all this information can be used to track people movements. This requires that a good privacy-preserving technique has to be applied when analysis such data. Unfortunately, the current proposals, as those presented in [45, 46], do not consider this aspect. However, the work in [46] is very interesting because studies user re-identification risks in GSM networks in the case user historical data is available to characterize the mobile users *a priori*.

6.2 Attack model and privacy by design solution

Given the above overview about the methodology for extracting global profiles and for computing a quantification of the different kinds of global profiles, now we analyze the privacy risks of the users.

We can identify three main phases in this process: (a) the extraction of the SCT profile for each user; (b) the extraction of global profiles; and (c) the quantification of different kinds of global profiles.

It is immediate to understand that the publication of the final result, i.e., the quantification of the global profiles cannot put at risk the individual privacy of any user because this information is a simple aggregation that does not contain any sensitive information about the single users. This means that an attacker by accessing this kind of data cannot infer any information about a user.

The first phase instead is more problematic for the individual privacy of users because requires to access the CDR data that contains all information about the user calls. In particular, for each user call we have the identifiers of the cell where the call starts and ends respectively and the date and time when the call starts, and its duration. The positional accuracy of cells is few hundred meters in a city [47] and when this information is combined with the time information all this information can help to track people movements. In [48] authors studied the user re-identification risks in GSM networks and showed that it is possible to identify a mobile user from CDR records and a pre-existing location profile, based on previous movements. In particular, one of the re-identification methods that they propose allows for the identification of around 80% of users. As a consequence, this kind of data can reveal sensitive user behavior and the telecommunication operator cannot release this data to the analyst without any privacy-preserving data transformation.

However, we observe that the only information that the analyst needs for computing the global profiles and their quantification is the set of SCT profiles; therefore, we propose an architecture where, the telecommunication operator computes the SCT profiles and then sends them to the analyst for the computation of the step (b) and (c). This solution avoids the access to the CDR logs for the analyst while provides to him the minimum information to performing the target analysis with correctness.

Now the question is: *Can an attacker infer private information about a user by accessing the set of SCT profiles? Is this form of data enough for protecting the individual privacy of each user in the system?* If the answer to this last question is yes, we could have both individual privacy protection and perfect quality of the analytical results.

First of all, we observe that a SCT profile can be seen as a spatio-temporal generalization of the CDR data of a user. Clearly, this form of data is more aggregated w.r.t. the CDR logs because it cannot reveal the history of the user movements, the number of calls and the exact day and time of each call. Moreover, this profile is constructed by considering a specific area such as a city therefore, it is impossible to infer where exactly the user went with a finer granularity. The only information that he can infer is that a specific user visited the city in a specific aggregated period. As an example, an attacker could understand that a given user went to Pisa during a specific week-end if the profiles that he was accessing are related to people in Pisa.

However, in the following we identify two possible attack models, based on the *linking attack*, that use two different background knowledge. Then, we simulate this two attacks on real-world data for showing the privacy protection provided by our schema.

Background knowledge 1. We assume that the attacker knows a set of locations visited by a user U where he called someone and the time of these calls. This means that he can build a SCT profile PB with this background knowledge, where $PB_{ij} = -1$ if the attacker does not have any information about the call activity of the user in the period (i,j) while $PB_{ij} = v$, with $v > 0$, if from the background knowledge he derives that the user was present in the area v times in the period (i,j).

Attack model 1. The attacker, who gains access to the set of SCT profiles, uses the background knowledge PB on the user U to match all the profiles that include PB. The set of matched profiles is the set $C = \{P \in \mathcal{P} | \forall PB_{ij} \geq 0, PB_{ij} \leq P_{ij}\}$. The probability of re-identification of the user U is $\frac{1}{|C|}$. Clearly, a greater number of candidates corresponds to a more privacy protection.

Background knowledge 2. In our study we also consider a different background knowledge. We assume that the attacker for some time periods (i,j) knows the exact number of times that a user U visited locations in the area of interest. This means that he can build a profile PB with this background knowledge, where $PB_{ij} = -1$ if the attacker does not have any information about the presence of the user U in the area of interest during the period (i,j) while $PB_{ij} = v$ with $v \geq 0$, if from the background knowledge he derives that the user was present in the area v times in the period (i,j). As an example, suppose an adversary knows that during the first week Mr. Smith went to Pisa in the time interval [08:00:00-18:59:59] only 4 times over 5 because Friday he was sick, Then, from this information he can construct a profile PB where $PB_{21} = 4$ while the other entries are equal to -1. Note, that in this case the attacker does not know if the user U did a call during his presence in the area of interest of the analysis and this implies that the malicious part does not know if the user U is represented in the set of profiles.

Attack model 2. The attacker, who gains access to the set of SCT profiles uses the background knowledge PB on the user U to select the set of candidate profiles $C = \{P \in \mathcal{P} | \forall PB_{ij} \geq 0, P_{i,j} \leq PB_{ij}\}$. The re-identification probability of the user U is $\frac{1}{|C|} \times Prob$, where $Prob$ is the probability that one of the profiles in $\mathcal{P}$ belongs to user U.

6.3 Privacy protection analysis

We performed a series of experiments on a real GSM dataset. We obtained a dataset of CDR logs in the Province of Pisa during the period from January 9th to February 8th 2012 reporting the activities of around 232k persons, for a total of 7.8M call records. Focusing on the urban area of the city of Pisa, we extracted the SCT profiles for the 63k users performing at least one call activity in the observation period. We then simulated two attacks according to the two attacking models above and measured the re-identification probability of each SCT profile.

The simulation is performed as follows: we generate a series of profiles PB according to the background knowledge 1 (background knowledge 2). These profiles are derived from the real user SCT profiles in the dataset. Then, we have performed the attack 1 (attack 2) on the set of profiles $\mathcal{P}$.

Concerning the attack 2 we have assumed that the adversary knows the exact number of times that the user visited locations in Pisa for each period (i,j), i.e., for all the 4 weeks in the profiles. Figure 9 shows the cumulative distribution of the re-identification probability. We found that in the worst case the probability of re-identification is 0.027% and only about 5% of users in the set of SCT profiles have this level of risk, while the other users

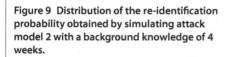

Figure 9 Distribution of the re-identification probability obtained by simulating attack model 2 with a background knowledge of 4 weeks.

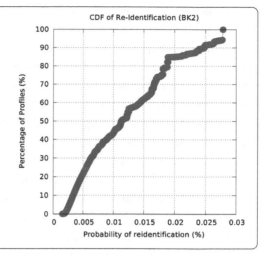

Figure 10 Distribution of the re-identification probability obtained by simulating attack model 1 with different levels of background knowledge.

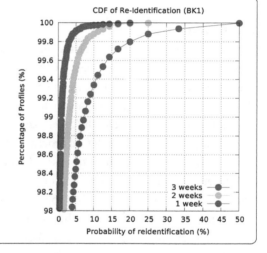

have a lower risk of privacy violation. This very high protection is due to the fact that with the background knowledge 2 (BK2) the attacker is not sure that the user is in the set of profiles that he is observing. However, even if we assume that he knows that the specific user is represented in the set of SCT profiles, the probability of re-identification is always low. We indeed have observed that the highest probability of re-identification in this case is 0.21%

Concerning the attack 1, that is based on a stronger background knowledge, we have assumed that the attacker knows the user call activities for a specific number of weeks and we have measured the probability to re-identify the user and infer his activities in the remaining weeks. Figure 10 shows the cumulative distribution of the re-identification probability for different levels of background knowledge: 1 week, 2 weeks and 3 weeks. As expected, when we increase the periods of observations of the adversary we have a worst privacy protection. However, when the attacker knows 1 week or 2 weeks of call activities of a specific users the probability of re-identification is always no more than 20% and 25% and this happens for about 0.01% of user in the profile data; 99.99% of users has a lower privacy risk. When we consider a observation period of 3 weeks the privacy protection decreases and for less than 0.1% of users the probability of re-identification is

50%, while for more than 99.9% of people the probability of re-identification is no more than 32%. Moreover, the 99% of users has a risk of re-identification less than about 7%. Clearly, here it is important to note that the background knowledge that we are taking into consideration is very strong. We have also measured the risk of re-identification assuming that the attacker knows the user call activities of different periods of the SCT profile. This kind of attack is similar to that one in [49] where authors discovered that 4 observations are enough to uniquely identify 95% of the individuals. In our experiments by using the SCT profiles instead of CDR logs, we have found that with 10 observations the probability of re-identification is less than 20% for all the users and about 99% of people has a risk of re-identification of about 1%. While if we consider 20 observations the situation is very similar to the case in which the attacker knows 3 weeks of calls of user in Figure 10.

The conclusion is that the illustrated process shows as by knowing the analysis to be performed on the data it is possible to transform the original data in a different form (by aggregations) and find a representation that both contains all the proprieties useful for obtaining a perfect analytical result and preserves the user privacy.

7 Conclusion

The potential impact of the big data analytics and social mining is high because it could generate enormous value to society. Unfortunately, often big data describes sensitive human activities and the privacy of people is always more at risk. The danger is increasing also thanks to the emerging capability to integrate diversified data. In this paper, we have introduced the articulation of the privacy-by-design in big data analytics and social mining for enabling the design of analytical processes that minimize the privacy harm, or even prevent the privacy harm. We have discussed how applying the privacy-by-design principle to four different scenarios showing that under suitable conditions is feasible to reach a good trade-off between data privacy and good quality of the data. We believe with the privacy-by-design principle social mining has the potential to provide a privacy-respectful social microscope, or socioscope, needed to observe the hidden mechanisms of socio-economic complexity.

Competing interests
The authors declare that they have no competing interests.

Authors' contributions
All authors contributed equally to the writing of this paper. All authors read and approved the final manuscript.

Acknowledgements
This work has been partially supported by EU FET-Open project DATA SIM (FP7-ICT 270833) and EU Project PETRA n. 609042 (FP7-SMARTCITIES-2013).

References
1. Batty M, Axhausen KW, Giannotti F, Pozdnoukhov A, Bazzani A, Wachowicz M, Ouzounis G, Portugali Y (2012) Smart cities of the future. Eur Phys J Spec Top 214(1):481-518
2. Brockmann D, Hufnagel L, Geisel T (2006) The scaling laws of human travel. Nature 439(7075):462-465
3. Giannotti F, Nanni M, Pedreschi D, Pinelli F, Renso C, Rinzivillo S, Trasarti R (2011) Unveiling the complexity of human mobility by querying and mining massive trajectory data. VLDB J 20(5):695-719
4. Gonzalez MC, Hidalgo CA, Barabasi A-L (2008) Understanding individual human mobility patterns. Nature 453(7196):779-782
5. Song C, Koren T, Wang P, Barabasi A-L (2010) Modelling the scaling properties of human mobility. Nat Phys 6(10):818-823
6. Song C, Qu Z, Blumm N, Barabási A-L (2010) Limits of predictability in human mobility. Science 327(5968):1018-1021
7. Wang D, Pedreschi D, Song C, Giannotti F, Barabási A-L (2011) Human mobility, social ties, and link prediction. In: KDD, pp 1100-1108

8. Balcan D, Gonçalves B, Hu H, Ramasco JJ, Colizza V, Vespignani A (2010) Modeling the spatial spread of infectious diseases: the global epidemic and mobility computational model. J Comput Sci 1(3):132-145
9. Colizza V, Barrat A, Barthelemy M, Valleron AJ, Vespignani A (2007) Modeling the worldwide spread of pandemic influenza: baseline case and containment interventions. PLoS Med 4(1):95-110
10. Colizza V, Barrat A, Barthélemy M, Vespignani A (2006) The role of the airline transportation network in the prediction and predictability of global epidemics. Proc Natl Acad Sci USA 103(7):2015-2020
11. Fumanelli L, Ajelli M, Manfredi P, Vespignani A, Merler S (2012) Inferring the structure of social contacts from demographic data in the analysis of infectious diseases spread. PLoS Comput Biol 8(9)
12. Gallos L, Havlin S, Kitsak M, Liljeros F, Makse H, Muchnik L, Stanley H (2010) Identification of influential spreaders in complex networks. Nat Phys 6(11):888-893
13. El Emam K, Cavoukian A (2014) De-identification protocols: essential for protecting privacy. http://www.privacybydesign.ca/content/uploads/2014/06/pbd-de-identifcation_essential.pdf
14. Abul O, Bonchi F, Nanni M (2008) Never walk alone: uncertainty for anonymity in moving objects databases. In: Proceedings of the 2008 IEEE 24th international conference on data engineering (ICDE), pp 376-385
15. Domingo-Ferrer J, Trujillo-Rasua R (2012) Microaggregation- and permutation-based anonymization of movement data. Inf Sci 208:55-80
16. Monreale A, Pedreschi D, Pensa RG (2010) Anonymity technologies for privacy-preserving data publishing and mining. In: Privacy-aware knowledge discovery: novel applications and new techniques, pp 3-33
17. Pensa RG, Monreale A, Pinelli F, Pedreschi D (2008) Pattern-preserving k-anonymization of sequences and its application to mobility data mining. In: PiLBA
18. Wong WK, Cheung DW, Hung E, Kao B, Mamoulis N (2007) Security in outsourcing of association rule mining. In: VLDB, pp 111-122
19. Cavoukian A (2000) Privacy design principles for an integrated justice system. Working paper. www.ipc.on.ca/index.asp?layid=86&fid1=318
20. Monreale A, Andrienko GL, Andrienko NV, Giannotti F, Pedreschi D, Rinzivillo S, Wrobel S (2010) Movement data anonymity through generalization. Trans Data Privacy 3(2):91-121
21. Giannotti F, Lakshmanan LVS, Monreale A, Pedreschi D, Wang WH (2013) Privacy-preserving mining of association rules from outsourced transaction databases. IEEE Syst J 7(3):385-395
22. Monreale A, Wang WH, Pratesi F, Rinzivillo S, Pedreschi D, Andrienko G, Andrienko N (2013) Privacy-preserving distributed movement data aggregation. In: AGILE. Springer, Berlin. doi:10.1007/978-3-319-00615-4_13
23. Furletti B, Gabrielli L, Renso C, Rinzivillo S (2012) Identifying users profiles from mobile calls habits. In: UrbComp'12, pp 17-24
24. (2010) Privacy by design resolution. In: International conference of data protection and privacy commissioners, Jerusalem, Israel, 27-29 october 2010
25. Article 29 data protection working party and working party on police and justice, the future of privacy: joint contribution to the consultation of the european commission on the legal framework for the fundamental right to protection of personal data. 02356/09/en, wp 168 (dec. 1, 2009)
26. European Data Protection Supervisor (Mar. 18, 2010) Opinion of the European data protection supervisor on promoting trust in the information society by fostering data protection and privacy
27. Federal Trade Commission (Bureau of Consumer Protection) (Dec. 2010) Preliminary staff report, protecting consumer privacy in an era of rapid change: a proposed framework for business and policy makers, at v, 41
28. Samarati P, Sweeney L (1998) Protecting privacy when disclosing information: k-anonymity and its enforcement through generalization and suppresion. In: Proc. of the IEEE symp. on research in security and privacy, pp 384-393
29. Samarati P, Sweeney L (1998) Generalizing data to provide anonymity when disclosing information (Abstract). In: PODS, p 188
30. Terrovitis M, Mamoulis N (2008) Privacy preservation in the publication of trajectories. In: Proc. of the 9th int. conf. on mobile data management (MDM)
31. Yarovoy R, Bonchi F, Lakshmanan LVS, Wang WH (2009) Anonymizing moving objects: how to hide a MOB in a crowd? In: EDBT, pp 72-83
32. Nergiz ME, Atzori M, Saygin Y, Güç B (2009) Towards trajectory anonymization: a generalization-based approach. Trans Data Privacy 2(1):47-75
33. Qiu L, Li Y, Wu X (2008) Protecting business intelligence and customer privacy while outsourcing data mining tasks. Knowl Inf Syst 17(1):99-120
34. Tai C, Yu PS, Chen M (2010) k-Support anonymity based on pseudo taxonomy for outsourcing of frequent itemset mining. In: KDD, pp 473-482
35. Molloy I, Li N, Li T (2009) On the (in)security and (im)practicality of outsourcing precise association rule mining. In: ICDM, pp 872-877
36. Dwork C, Mcsherry F, Nissim K, Smith A (2006) Calibrating noise to sensitivity in private data analysis. In: Proceedings of the 3rd theory of cryptography conference. Springer, Berlin, pp 265-284
37. Beimel A, Nissim K, Omri E (2008) Distributed private data analysis: simultaneously solving how and what. In: CRYPTO, pp 451-468
38. Chan T-HH, Shi E, Song D (2012) Optimal lower bound for differentially private multi-party aggregation. In: ESA, pp 277-288
39. Rastogi V, Nath S (2010) Differentially private aggregation of distributed time-series with transformation and encryption. In: SIGMOD, pp 735-746
40. Shi E, Chan T-HH, Rieffel EG, Chow R, Song D (2011) Privacy-preserving aggregation of time-series data. In: NDSS
41. Dwork C (2006) Differential privacy. In: Bugliesi M, Preneel B, Sassone V, Wegener I (eds) Automata, languages and programming. Lecture notes in computer science, vol 4052. Springer, Berlin, pp 1-12
42. Kohonen T (2001) Self-organizing maps. Springer series in information sciences, vol 30
43. Golle P, Partridge K (2009) On the anonymity of home/work location pairs. In: Pervasive computing, pp 390-397
44. Zang H, Bolot J (2011) Anonymization of location data does not work: a large-scale measurement study. In: Proceedings of the 17th annual international conference on mobile computing and networking, pp 145-156. ACM

45. Croft NJ, Olivier MS (2006) Sequenced release of privacy accurate call data record information in a GSM forensic investigation. ISSA, Sandton, South Africa
46. De Mulder Y, Danezis G, Batina L, Preneel B (2008) Identification via location-profiling in GSM networks. In: Proceedings of the 7th ACM workshop on privacy in the electronic society, pp 23-32. ACM
47. Trevisani E, Vitaletti A (2004) Cell-ID location technique, limits and benefits: an experimental study. In: WMCSA'04, pp 51-60. IEEE
48. De Mulder Y, Danezis G, Batina L, Preneel B (2008) Identification via location-profiling in GSM networks. In: WPES'08, pp 23-32. ACM
49. de Montjoye Y-A, Hidalgo CA, Verleysen M, Blondel VD (2013) Unique in the crowd: the privacy bounds of human mobility. Scientific reports 3

5

Unveiling patterns of international communities in a global city using mobile phone data

Paolo Bajardi[1], Matteo Delfino[2], André Panisson[2], Giovanni Petri[2] and Michele Tizzoni[2]*

*Correspondence:
michele.tizzoni@isi.it
[2]ISI Foundation, via Alassio 11/C,
Torino, 10126, Italy
Full list of author information is
available at the end of the article

Abstract

We analyse a large mobile phone activity dataset provided by Telecom Italia for the *Telecom Big Data Challenge* contest. The dataset reports the international country codes of every call/SMS made and received by mobile phone users in Milan, Italy, between November and December 2013, with a spatial resolution of about 200 meters. We first show that the observed spatial distribution of international codes well matches the distribution of international communities reported by official statistics, confirming the value of mobile phone data for demographic research. Next, we define an entropy function to measure the heterogeneity of the international phone activity in space and time. By comparing the entropy function to empirical data, we show that it can be used to identify the city's hotspots, defined by the presence of points of interests. Eventually, we use the entropy function to characterize the spatial distribution of international communities in the city. Adopting a topological data analysis approach, we find that international mobile phone users exhibit some robust clustering patterns that correlate with basic socio-economic variables. Our results suggest that mobile phone records can be used in conjunction with topological data analysis tools to study the geography of migrant communities in a global city.

Keywords: mobile phone data; entropy; urban geography

1 Introduction

A city is a complex system shaped by the continuously evolving interactions among its inhabitants and visitors. The recent availability of a profusion of data generated by human behavior and collected through pervasive sensors has motivated a strong and renewed interest for the study of urban spaces, building upon an established research tradition [1, 2]. Indeed, the new possibilities opened up by the current technological advances in data gathering and processing have led to the definition of a new age for the *Science of Cities* [3].

Nowadays, through the analysis of large amounts of real-time user-generated data it is possible to obtain new insights into the living conditions of a city and understand its transformations. Recently, such research has gained great popularity leading to a number of studies that leverage on urban data to monitor a city's life and structure. In particular, a major finding in this field has been the discovery that many diverse socio-economic properties of cities, from personal income to gasoline consumption, follow a power law function of population size with scaling exponents that fall into distinct universality classes [4–8]. Analogously, similar scaling relations have been shown to hold for the social connectivity of individuals in a city [9]. Such empirical evidence has further motivated the development of several theoretical attempts to explain the observed regularities of cities [10–13] paving the way to a - yet to come - scientific theory of cities [14].

Within this context, studies of human behavior in the urban space have been strongly promoted by the availability of mobile phones call detail records (CDRs) of millions of users in different countries. Mobile phone data have been shown to be an invaluable source of information to extract individual mobility patterns at a high spatial resolution [15, 16]. Using mobile phone data, it has been possible to study migratory and commuting movements, both in industrialized [17] and developing countries [18], with applications ranging from disaster management [19, 20] to infectious disease epidemiology [21–23]. Moving beyond the analysis of human movements, recent works have shown that mobile phone data can be useful to study metropolitan land use [24–28] and, more in general, can provide some quantitative measures to classify cities in terms of their polycentrism, by identifying a city's hotspots and monitoring their stability over time [29].

In this paper, we deal with the study of urban spaces through the analysis of mobile phone records by focusing on a specific subset of mobile phone users, that is those with strong international links, which typically charecterise short and long term migrant communities and those travelling to a city as tourists or for work. More precisely, we analyse a high-resolution dataset of mobile phone records collected in Milan, which has the most populous metropolitan area in Italy, that reports the international code of all calls and text messages sent and received by a user over a two-month period. Based on such call records, collected at a very high spatial and temporal resolution, we define an entropy function that measures the level of heterogeneity in the number of distinct countries - identified by their international phone code - that are present in the activity record of a city's neighborhood. By analysing the spatial and temporal features of such entropy function, we aim to identify locations that attract the most visitors and characterize how international communities occupy and make use of the urban spaces.

In particular, here we show and discuss how an entropy measure of the phone activity can be used to: (i) recognize the most attractive locations for tourists and visitors in the city, as indicated by the presence of point of interests; (ii) characterize the spatial distribution of diverse communities, recognizing - in conjunction with information obtained from topological data analysis - the different use of the metropolitan area made by visitors and residents. Additionally, we discuss how our proposed method can be advantageous with respect to only using the volume of mobile phone activity for similar analyses.

The paper is structured as follows: in Section 2 we describe the main features of the dataset under study; in Section 3 we link the diversity arising from mobile phones activity aggregates to the population diversity of Milan; in Section 4 we introduce an entropy measure to quantify the diversity of mobile phones activity and present the results obtained by analysing its properties; in Section 5 we describe how a topological data analysis based on persistent homology is able to discriminate between resident and visiting foreigners in the city, once a spatial entropy-activity distribution has been properly defined. Finally, we conclude and discuss our results.

The Python code that has been used to perform the data analysis of this work is available at the following repository: http://github.com/micheletizzoni/Bajardi-et-al-EPJDS-2015.

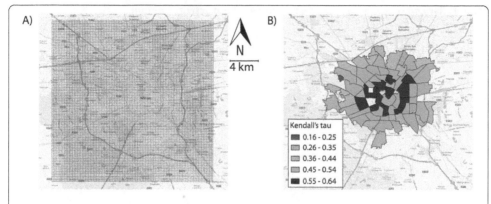

Figure 1 Milan grid and spatial distribution of foreign residents. (A) The map shows the metropolitan area of Milan, Italy, and the area covered by the reference grid. **(B)** The map shows the neighborhoods (NILs) of the Milan municipality. Each neighborhood is color coded according to the Kendall's tau correlation coefficient between the nationalities reported by census and those recorded in the mobile phone dataset.

2 Dataset description

The dataset has been provided by Telecom Italia in the context of the 'Telecom Big Data Challenge' [30] and contains the mobile phone activity records - including both SMS and calls made or received - of all users in the Milan area (Italy) during a time span of two months, from November 1 to December 31, 2013. Data is aggregated over a 10 minutes interval and is geolocalized on a grid of 100×100 squares covering the city metropolitan area with a resolution of about 235 meters (map shown in Figure 1A). Traffic volume data has been provided with the same arbitrary units for text messages and calls. In this way, the provider assured both quantities to be directly comparable.

In our study, we focused on a specific information provided with the dataset, that is, the list of international country phone codes that are present in the activity record of each cell, with their corresponding traffic volume, for every 10-minutes time slice. As expected, the vast majority (97% of the total traffic) of the mobile phone activity is exchanged between Italian phone numbers; there is however a relatively small but very heterogeneous fraction of calls involving foreign phone numbers. During the three-month period, 221 different country codes appeared in the activity record indicating the presence of many foreigners in the city. Indeed, Milan is a diverse city with a long immigration history and a number of communities of foreigners originating from several developing countries. Moreover, Milan is a popular destination for tourist and business reasons, with important cultural attractions and hosts the headquarters of several multinational companies (the Province of Milan alone accounts for about 10% of the national GDP).

3 Mapping the diversity of mobile phones activity

Following the above considerations, it is reasonable to argue that mobile phones data could be used as a proxy to measure the diversity of the resident population living in the city without having to resort to census data. It is clear, however, that mobile phones data accounts also for individuals who are not permanent residents and, therefore, cannot be tracked by census. Furthermore, the estimation of the population diversity using mobile phones data will be biased by different usage patterns between different demographic groups [31].

Table 1 Ranked nationalities by census and by calling activity volume

Rank	Census population	Calling activity
1	Philippines	Egypt
2	Egypt	Bangladesh
3	China	Switzerland
4	Peru	China
5	Sri Lanka	Ukraine
6	Ecuador	France
7	Romania	United Kingdom
8	Morocco	Sri Lanka
9	Ukraine	Philippines
10	Bangladesh	Romania
11	Albania	Russia
12	El Salvador	Germany
13	France	Spain
14	Brazil	Senegal
15	Moldova	Ecuador

To quantify the extent to which mobile phones data can be used as a proxy for estimating the diversity of the city population, we compared the list of countries ranked by their cumulative calling activity records with the nationalities of residents ranked by their prevalence as reported in the local census in the year 2012 [32]. As shown in Table 1, 9 out of the top 15 countries ranked by phone traffic volume are also present in the top nationalities according to the census data. The Kendall tau correlation between the ranked vectors of nationalities equals 0.69 ($p < 0.01$), showing a strong and significant correlation between the two rankings. To further investigate the correlation between mobile phones and census, we also compared the rankings of the different nationalities emerging from the two datasets at a finer spatial resolution.

Aggregating the cells at the NIL level (namely, *Nuclei di identità locale* - a subdivision of the urban area comprising 88 neighborhoods) and summing the whole traffic over the entire period of observation, we built for every NIL a vector of country-specific activities. Neighborhoods for which no census data was available (mostly parks and peripheral neighborhoods) were dropped, leaving a total of 66 NILs. We then evaluated for each NIL the Kendall's tau rank correlation coefficient between the sorted list of resident foreigner population and the sorted vector of mobile phones traffic from/to foreign countries. Each test led to statistically significant correlations ($p < 0.01$), with the exception of one NIL (the least populous one) for which no significant correlation was found between mobile phones and census rankings. For each of the remaining neighborhoods, as shown in Figure 1B, the Kendall's tau value was larger than 0.3. More specifically, it was larger than 0.4 for 55 (83%) of the NILs with median value 0.48 and 95% reference range [0.32-0.69], showing that mobile phones data can be used as a first order proxy to study the distribution of the resident foreign population even at a finer spatial resolution.

4 Entropy of mobile phone activity

Raw activity aggregates, although useful as shown in the previous section, suffer from noise and biases originating from different kinds of overlapping activities from residential, tourist and working centers. Furthermore, activity aggregates fail to convey information about the specificity and the diversity of the activity at the finest spatial and temporal levels.

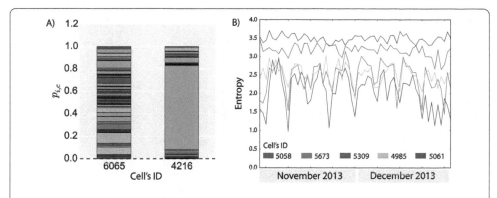

Figure 2 Entropy of international mobile phone activity. (**A**) The plot shows the distribution of the calling activity, over the whole reporting period, for two specific grid cells. For each cell, a stacked bar chart displays how the calling activity is distributed over different country codes, denoted by different colors. (**B**) Entropy time series for five selected grid cells, from November 1 to December 31, 2013.

For these reasons, following previous approaches [33] we defined an entropy measure to quantify the heterogeneity of a single cell activity pattern and infer specific spatial and temporal characteristics of the corresponding urban area.

4.1 Definition

We define an entropy function on every cell of the Milan grid to measure the heterogeneity of the mobile phone activity in terms of the country codes that are present in the cell's temporal activity record. As a matter of notation, we represent the raw activity values as a time-dependent multi-dimensional matrix $A_{i,c}(t)$ where i runs over the grid ids, c refers to the country where the traffic was directed to or originating from, and t is the temporal dimension that can be tuned to different granularities (hourly, daily, etc.). Omitting the temporal dependency, we define the probability of observing a mobile phone activity related to a given country c in a cell i as $p_{i,c} = A_{i,c}/\sum_c A_{i,c}$ and thus the entropy as:

$$S_i = -\sum_c p_{i,c} \cdot \log(p_{i,c}). \tag{1}$$

As sketched in Figure 2A, a cell where the activity is evenly distributed among many countries will have a large entropy value suggesting that the phone traffic origin or destination is highly unpredictable, while if most of the activity is related to one or few countries only, the entropy will assume lower values. In the following we will use different temporal aggregations, considering both the activity over the whole period or on a daily basis, resulting in an overall entropy value for a given cell or in an entropy time series, respectively. Figure 2B shows some examples of daily entropy time series. From the plot it is possible to distinguish between two main qualitative behaviors of the entropy function: on the one hand, some cells display a high and steady entropy value over the course of the observed period (e.g. cells 5058 and 5061), on the other hand, some cells display a lower entropy value with distinct weekly pattern, where entropy gets smaller during weekends (e.g. cells 5309 and 4985). The first type of behavior is usually found in busy or central areas of the city, such as the central railway station, the Linate airport or in proximity of tourist attractions. The latter type of behavior is more typical of strictly residential and working areas, such as the University of Milan and the city outskirts.

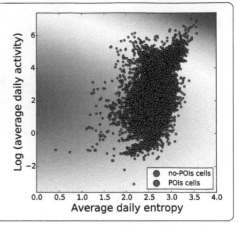

Figure 3 Entropy and points of interest. Correlation between average daily activity and entropy and the presence of points of interests in a cell. Points are scatterplot for each cell of the Milan grid ($r = 0.36$, $p < 10^{-4}$) and are color coded according to the presence of POIs (red) or not (blue). In the background, a color gradient describes the values of a decision function based on a SVM model with RBF kernel (parameters: $C = 1$ and $\gamma = 10^{-2}$, estimated via 3-fold cross-validation). Red corresponds to positive decision, i.e. presence of POIs, and blue to negative decision.

4.2 Entropy and point of interests

A way to corroborate the hypothesis that high entropy areas can identify the busiest and most attractive locations is to compare the entropy distributions of different locations against an independent measure of their importance. To this aim, we considered the presence of point of interests (POIs) according to the popular travel website TripAdvisor (http://www.tripadvisor.com) as a proxy to measure a location's attractiveness. More precisely, we mapped all the locations that are listed as 'Attractions in Milan' by TripAdvisor [34] on the georeferenced grid and measured the average daily entropy of the cells where at least 1 point of interest was located. We found that the two quantities, number of POIs in a cell and its average daily entropy, are positively correlated (Spearman's correlation coefficient $r = 0.36$, $p < 10^{-4}$). Furthermore, the average daily entropy distribution of the cells without points of interest and the entropy distribution of the cells with at least one point of interest are significantly different (2-sample KS test at 1% level), with the latter being skewed towards higher entropy values (see Figure S1 in the Additional file 1).

It is immediate to notice, however, that the cells having at least one point of interest are only 219 out of 10,000, and only 6 cells have 6 or more points of interest in their area (Figure S1A in the Additional file 1). Moreover, the average daily activity is also correlated with the presence of POIs in a cell (Spearman's correlation coefficient $r = 0.49$, $p < 10^{-4}$), indicating that attractive locations are also trivially characterized by a high calling volume. To examine how the entropy measure can add some useful information to this picture, we analysed the distributions of both daily activity and daily entropy in the presence or absence of points of interests. As shown in Figure 3, we found that the correlation between phone activity volume and entropy is not trivial and, more remarkably, most of the locations with points of interests (in red) are characterized by both high entropy and high activity and clustered in a relatively small region of the activity-entropy space. To provide a quantitative measure of the information added by the entropy, we trained a classification model based on a support vector machine (SVM) to automatically identify a cell with POIs. The values of the decision function are shown in Figure 3 as a background blue-to-red gradient. The decision boundary, determined by the line that separates the positive values (in red) from the negative values (in blue) of the decision function, is a nonlinear combination of both activity and entropy, and is able to classify with good accuracy the cells with attractive locations. Although the model's scores are not very relevant in this context since most of the false positives (blue points in the red area) are in fact cells adjacent to other attractive cells, we report that the results of a model trained with both activity and entropy are better (ROC AUC 0.93) than the results obtained by a model trained with just activity (ROC AUC 0.79). In the end, our results indicate that the entropy function of Equation (1) not only represents a reliable measure of a location attractiveness but could be effectively used to refine those methods that identify the hotspots of a city, based only on the raw activity volume.

4.3 Entropy outliers

Given the definition of entropy provided by Equation (1), for every cell i and for every time step t (in the following, a daily resolution is chosen) we are able to measure a certain entropy value and starting from the original dataset we recover 10,000 entropy time series. By calculating a modified z-score where mean and standard deviation are replaced by the median and the median absolute deviation values [35], we are able to systematically detect the days when the entropy profile shows a significantly different behavior than usual. An entropy outlier may be triggered by an unexpected increase or decrease in the mobile phone activity inwards/towards foreign locations. The rationale behind the automatic detection of outliers is to use the entropy level as a fingerprint to characterize an urban area, where the outlying points indicate some exceptional events occurring in that location.

In Figure 4A the fraction of detected outliers is shown for every day of observation. An overall pattern emerges: during the weekends and Christmas holidays, the number of cells with an exceptional activity profile increases. In Figure 4B we observe that less than one fourth of the cells has an unexpected activity during the two months period of observation, and among them, more than 70% shows only one outlier. On the other hand, there are 32 cells with 5 or more outlying days in terms of entropy profiles. Such cells are located either

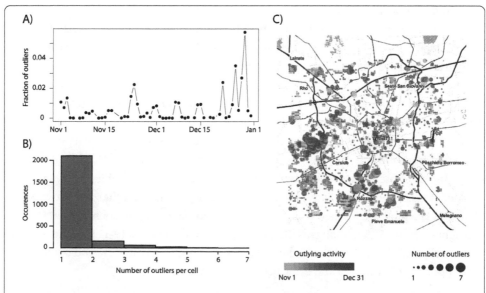

Figure 4 Entropy outliers. (**A**) Fraction of cells that display an entropy outlier value, measured in terms of a modified median z-score, over the period of observation. (**B**) Distribution of the number of outlying days per cell. (**C**) Georeferenced outlying activity on the Milano area. Bigger circles represent cells with a larger number of outlying days while the cyan-to-purple color indicates the outlying period from early November to late December.

in low-activity areas, which are more prone to entropy fluctuations, or close to important crossroads probably representative of a genuine special activity.

Beyond the overall patterns, we georeferenced the outlying activity cells and we mapped in Figure 4C both the median outlying day per cell and the number of outlying days per cell. The majority of darker cells - corresponding to late December - remarks the abundance of outlying activity close to the Christmas holidays, probably generated by the increasing presence of tourists and by the disruption of the typical workday patterns.

4.4 Monitoring large-scale events

Here, we demonstrate how it is also possible to leverage on the raw mobile phone's activity to monitor large-scale events in real-time. On December 11, 2013 an important football match between AC Milan and the Dutch team of AFC Ajax was hosted in Milan. Analysing the mobile phone data, we found some entropy outliers (see Figure S2 in the Additional file 1) close to the airport, the stadium and few other places around the city. In order to investigate the crowd displacements at a finer temporal scale, we focused on the raw mobile phones activity (sum of calls and sms) related to traffic from/to the Netherlands aggregated over 1-hour intervals. For every time interval, the most active 50 cells are shown on the map (Figure 5), color coded according to the recorded activity with an orange-to-blue gradient associated to low-to-high traffic. Since the mobile phone activity clearly follows strong circadian patterns, every snapshot is normalized on the hourly activity and therefore the maps describe the geolocated predominant presence of Dutch communication for every time window and the magnitude of such activity can not be directly compared among different maps.

Assuming that the majority of mobile phones activity from/to the Netherlands is linked to the presence of Dutch supporters, it is possible to monitor the geo-temporal movements of the crowd in the urban area. Before 6 am the recorded activity accounts for less than 4% of the total daily activity and the cells are quite scattered over the city with some hotspots close to the railway stations. At 6 am, the most active cells are those close to the Linate airport, Porta Genova and Central railway stations, thus registering the arrival of the first Ajax's supporters. At 7 am a large activity is also registered on the top-left corner of the Milano grid, suggesting that a group of supporters is probably reaching the city from the Malpensa airport that is located on that side of the region, as well as a sustained activity still registered at Linate and at the several railway stations. During the central hours of the day, most of the supporters were probably visiting the city center and indeed the activity is scattered over that area. Approaching the match at 6-7 pm, a strong activity is observed at the underground stations close to the stadium and the stadium itself. During the hour preceding the match, most of the activity is located at the stadium while a very localized hotspot is observed at the San Carlo Borromeo Hospital and another one close to the Niguarda Hospital: we learned from the news that six Ajax supporters had been stabbed in a fight with AC Milan hooligans [36]. During the football match (9-11 pm) the majority of the activity is observed at the stadium, as expected, and soon after the end of the match the supporters left the area and came back to the city center.

5　Topological data analysis of international communities

Previous work exploited individual geolocated digital traces [37] to study the different prominence and distribution of international communities within an English-speaking environment. The most intuitive proxy for migrant communities is the aggregated call and

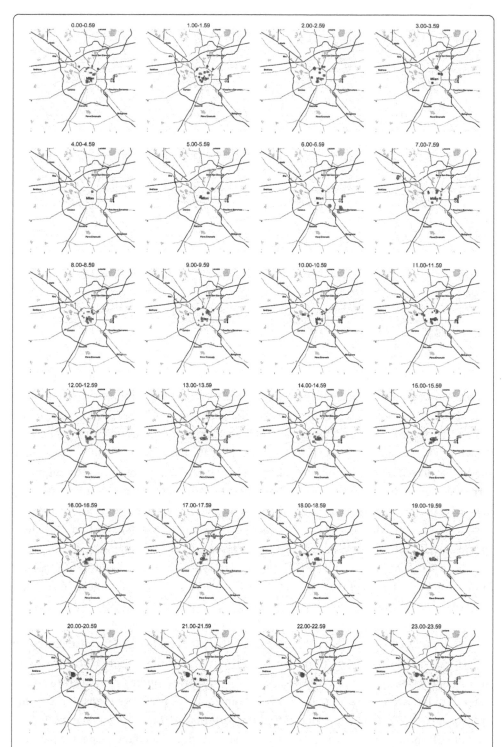

Figure 5 Phone activity during an international football match. Most active 50 cells of mobile phones traffic from/to the Netherlands on December 11, 2013. Orange-to-blue color gradient corresponds to low-to-high activity. Every hourly map is normalized by the corresponding total hourly activity.

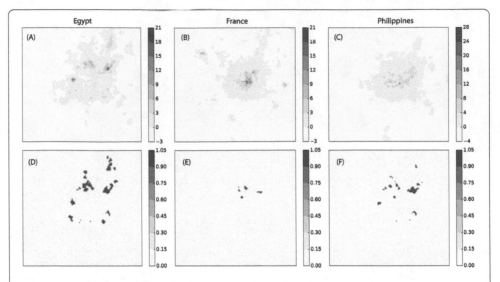

Figure 6 Country-specific activity/entropy maps. Top: maps of the calling activity volume for three different international country codes: Egypt (**A**), France (**B**) and Philippines (**C**). The activity is reported here in z-score units relative to the distribution of each country. Bottom: locations with high activity and low entropy for Egypt (**D**), France (**E**) and Philippines (**F**).

sms activity of a cell to/from another country, the natural implication being that a large activity toward a country c highlights the presence of a substantial population of nationals of c. However, activity alone hardly produces informative results. In fact, the scale of activity can vary wildly across different cells and therefore a large total activity in a cell might drown relevant signals from others. Figure 6A helps illustrating this point. Despite some variability driven by the number of country-specific foreigners, we find a common pattern that highlights the importance of the city center. Maps of activity are indeed strongly biased by the busiest places in terms of tourist attraction, business, etc. This in turn underlines the second shortcoming of using activity alone: activity is not able to discern how specific a cell's activity is to a certain country. Entropy, on the contrary, quantifies exactly this disparity. A cell that can be reliably associated with a country should thus display a low entropy, which implies that most of its activity belongs to a small number of countries, and large activity toward the selected country.

For each country c, we considered only the cells i that had activity $A_{i,c} > \mu_{A_c} + \sigma_{A_c}$ and entropy $z_{S_i} < \bar{z}$, where μ_{A_c} and σ_{A_c} are the first and second moment of the distribution of activity restricted to country c over all cells, and z_{S_i} is the entropy z-score of the ith cell. In the rest of the paper we used a threshold value $\bar{z} = -2$, corresponding to an entropy that is 2 standard deviations smaller than the average entropy. We performed sensitivity testing by varying $\bar{z} \in [-3, -0.5]$ and we found that the patterns are robust under changes in $\bar{z}$.

Figure 6B shows that imposing these two constraints peculiar country-specific patterns emerge. Direct observation points to two main types of configurations:

- (single or multiple) spatially coherent clusters;
- spatially dispersed and annular clusters, with possible branching structures.

It is tempting to try to characterize quantitatively the similarity between configurations of different countries and possibly use them to cluster countries according to them. However, the intrinsic noise in the dataset and the variability in the configurations' shapes require robust shape descriptors that allow for stretching, rotations, thinning and translations.

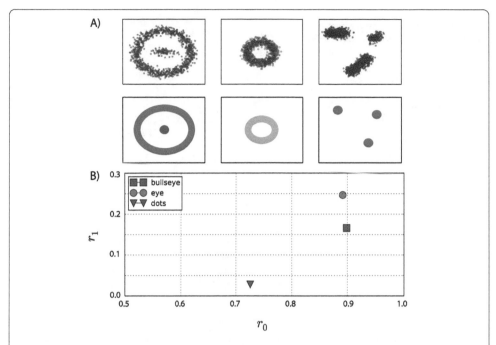

Figure 7 Classification method based on persistent homology. (A) Point clouds defined in metrical spaces can be studied effectively through the features of associated simplicial approximations. In particular, from the actual data sample (top row) it is possible to extract their coarse-grained representations that preserve their homological properties (bottom row). **(B)** To each recovered shape, we can then associate a pair (r_0, r_1) describing the shape's spatial coherency and circularity and use this information to classify the original datasets.

Topological features are one example of this kind of descriptors. Various recently appeared methods are able to characterize in a robust way the mesoscopic features of data spaces. They are based on ideas coming from computational topology and were introduced in the context of data analysis by [38–40]. They have been used in biology [41–44], brain functional networks [45], shape recognition [46–48], sensor network coverage [49] and complex networks [50, 51].

Figure 7A provides an ideal example of this type of shape classification: given a point cloud (Figure 7A top row), the features that are topologically detectable in two dimensions are its connectedness and circularity. In this way, it is possible to discern structures that are qualitatively different such as the three examples shown (Figure 7A bottom row). Persistent homology [38] - a parametrised version of homology for data spaces - provides the main tool to detect and quantify these differences between point clouds.

For a given data space, persistent homology yields a description of its homological structure in terms of the properties of the homology generators along a series of successive approximations of the real dataset. For our purposes however, it will be sufficient to focus on two simple derived quantities, r_0 and r_1.

The former, r_0, measures the spatial coherency of the point cloud, in terms of the difference between the point cloud's diameter and the radius of the point neighborhoods necessary to obtain a single connected component. We normalize r_0 by the diameter in order to obtain a value in $(0, 1)$.

The latter, r_1, similarly conveys the large scale circularity of the point cloud by considering the ratio of the two largest circles obtained by gluing neighborhoods together. Since

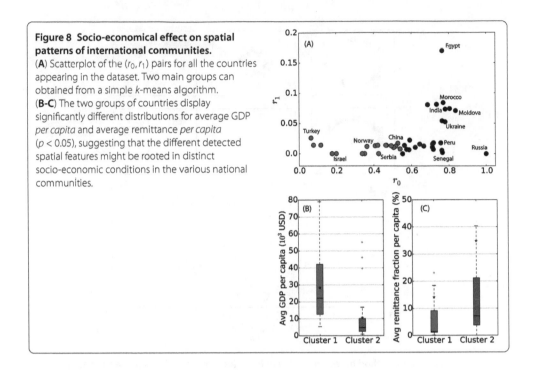

Figure 8 Socio-economical effect on spatial patterns of international communities.
(**A**) Scatterplot of the (r_0, r_1) pairs for all the countries appearing in the dataset. Two main groups can obtained from a simple k-means algorithm.
(**B-C**) The two groups of countries display significantly different distributions for average GDP *per capita* and average remittance *per capita* ($p < 0.05$), suggesting that the different detected spatial features might be rooted in distinct socio-economic conditions in the various national communities.

the formal definition these quantities requires some mathematical technicalities, we refer the interested reader to Section 3 in the Additional file 1. However, it is easy to see that the (r_0, r_1) pairs calculated for the three examples are clearly distinct (Figure 7B) and correspond to intuitive description: the *bullseye* and the *eye* examples have larger spatial decoherence and circularity than the *dots* example, with the *eye* having the largest circularity, due to the *bullseye*'s central cluster marring its symmetry.

We repeated the same analysis on entropy-activity filtered maps for all the countries, obtaining the complete list of (r_0, r_1).

In line with the naive observations of Figure 6, we used a simple k-means clustering ($k = 2$) to single out the two emerging clusters: one containing countries characterised by low values of both ratios, the second containing those with large values of r_0 and varying values of r_1. It is interesting to note that the two groups also appear to correspond to two different socio-economic demographics. We found indeed that countries corresponding to small r_0 and r_1 have significantly larger average GDP *per capita* (2-sample KS = 0.7, p-value < 0.05) and lower remittances ratios [52] (2-sample KS = 0.46, p-value < 0.05) as compared to countries corresponding to larger r_0 and r_1 values (Figure 8B and 8C), suggesting an interpretation of the detected spatial patterns in terms of the different types of migrations to Milan (e.g. low income labour migration versus cultural migration). Moreover, the results do not seem to be sensitive to different choice of the entropy threshold, since we found that the results are robust for a range of choices of z-threshold value ($\bar{z} \in [-3, -0.5]$) as shown in Figures S3 and S4 of the Additional file 1. Our approach provides a basis for further data-driven and time-resolved analyses of the factors that shape the spatial properties of migrant communities in a city, in addition to the standard macroscopic push-pull description [53].

6 Discussion

In the past few years, the availability of detailed user-generated data has unveiled a tremendous potential for the development of computational social sciences [54]. A fundamental contribution to this research field has derived from the analysis of mobile phones data, which has been proved to be an important source of information to study how people move [15, 55] and interact [56, 57], especially in a urban environment [24, 58–60].

In this work, we have studied a highly resolved dataset containing the international country codes of millions of anonymized and geo-referenced records of calls that have been made or received during a two-month period in the city of Milan, Italy. We focused our attention on the heterogeneity of the international codes appearing in the dataset in order to extract meaningful information about the spatial distribution and the land use related to the presence of migrant communities or tourist hubs in the city.

First, by comparing the frequency and the spatial aggregation of the international country codes to official census data, we have shown that mobile phones data can be used as a proxy for estimating the ranking of foreign residents of Milan up to the NILs level. This result generally confirms the value of mobile phones as a tool for demographic research [61, 62] and suggests the possibility to analyse mobile phone traffic to infer the population distribution of foreigners with a higher temporal and spatial resolutions than those typical of census surveys. In this respect, the advantage of using mobile phone data would be the relatively low cost compared to traditional expensive and time consuming surveys. On the other hand, mobile phone data can not be assumed to be fully representative of the population because there are differences in the use of mobile phones across demographic groups [31]. Similar biases arise from the fact that mobile phones include individuals who are not permanent residents. A solution to overcome the biases related to such issues could be mixing the analysis of large-scale mobile phone datasets with the collection of small-sample surveys [61].

The use of an entropy measure to quantify the diversity of behavioral patterns and social interactions and the analysis of its relations with socio-demographic attributes has been the subject of previous studies [33, 63]. Here, we used it as a complementary measure to characterize the metropolitan spaces based on the heterogeneity of the country codes that appear in the calling records. Previous works showed that a larger diversity of social interactions was linked to high socio-economic levels [33]. Here, we found that both high entropy and high calling activity identify the most attractive locations of a city. In particular, through a machine learning algorithm, we showed how the entropy function can be used to distinguish between those places that have a large calling volume but are not points of interests and those that are attractive for international visitors. This result suggests that the entropy function could be used in conjunction with more sophisticated methods [29] to quantify how much foreigners contribute to the importance of a city's hotspot, distinguishing between locations that attract the natives and those that attract visitors. Moreover, our findings emphasize the fact that phone activity alone is not completely informative in the case of hotspots recognition. On the other hand, while the entropy is able to provide insights into the use of urban spaces, we also showed that mobile phone activity can be effectively used to monitor in real-time city-scale mass events. In this context, our results confirm previous works where mobile phones have been used to infer the crowd density during mass gatherings [64]. In our case, we demonstrated how mobile phone data can provide very specific spatial and temporal trajectories of visitors from a given country (the Netherlands, in our case) during a mass gathering event. Similar situations are typical of large sport, artistic and religious events, whose management requires large coordinated efforts. The analysis of the football match also hinted at the possible use of entropy outliers to automatically detect unusual events. This is, however, only an hypothesis that needs further testing on a larger dataset to be verified.

The proposed characterization of different urban areas by means of an entropy function provides a helpful description of the locations where a large diversity of people tend to gather together. In our work, we outlined two distinct behaviors that can identify either tourist places, where many point of interests attract different foreigners, or residential areas where migrant communities are well consolidated. By using a topological classification based on persistent homology, we uncovered some significant regularities in the shape of foreign communities, as identified by a combination of low-entropy and high-activity cells. When described in terms of their topological indices, the nationalities associated to the call's destinations and sources outside Italy are clustered into two main groups. The first comprises low-income countries, whose topological spatial pattern displays a strong cyclic spatial distribution. The second group is formed by higher income countries, whose spatial distribution is scattered in small areas over the city. These results indicate that migrant communities from low income labour countries tend to aggregate in cohesive spatial structures that populate the city's residential areas, mainly scattered around the city centre. On the other hand, communities associated with higher income countries tend to reflect mostly tourist movements or highly specialized labour associated with central, high-entropy urban areas. In both cases, their spatial patterns are expected to be sparser and less structured. Our findings are in the direction predicted by the spatial assimilation theory [65] and confirm the empirical observation that different socio-economic migrant conditions can show distinct spatial clustering patterns [66]. In this context, our work opens the way to a completely new approach to the geography of immigrant communities within a city, based on topological data analysis, which could help to uncover a more refined classification for such communities.

Further research is needed to fully explore the potential applications of the proposed method and validate it. First of all, our work is limited by the fact that the dataset is restricted to one city. Thus, an extension of our analysis to different cities, both in developed and developing countries, is needed. Even if strong regularities are observed across cities [5], each city has its own peculiar structure, such as being monocentric or polycentric [67], and we may expect such features to affect the spatial distribution of the entropy function. Also, the attractiveness for foreigners may significantly vary across cities in the same country, leading to a more or less important contribution of foreign country codes to the mobile phone activity. In general, we expect our results to hold for large and diverse metropolitan areas, as in the case of Milan. Finally, our work is affected by the limited period over which data has been collected, because a two-month record is not sufficient to uncover long-term trends in the activity of users. In particular, a longer time frame is necessary to better define the presence of outliers in the entropy distribution and possibly link them with the recognition of unusual events.

Additional material

> **Additional file 1: Supplementary information.** Correlation between entropy and points of interest. Entropy outliers during the football match Ajax-Milan. Mathematical details of the persistent homology. Sensitivity analysis on the clustering of international communities.

Competing interests
The authors declare that they have no competing interests.

Authors' contributions
PB, MD, AP, GP and MT conceived and designed the study, carried out the data analysis and drafted the manuscript. All authors read and approved the final manuscript.

Author details
[1]Aizoon Technology Consulting, via Po 14, Torino, 10123, Italy. [2]ISI Foundation, via Alassio 11/C, Torino, 10126, Italy.

Acknowledgements
The authors acknowledge Telecom Italia for providing the original dataset. The work has been partially supported by the EC FET-Proactive Project MULTIPLEX (Grant No. 317532) to MT and the EC FET-Proactive Project TOPDRIM (Grant No. 318121) to GP. We gratefully acknowledge Marco Quaggiotto for help with GIS mapping and Joanna Cordero for helpful comments.

References
1. Batty M, Longley P (1994) Fractal cities. Academic Press, San Diego
2. Fujita M, Krugman PR, Venables AJ (1999) The spatial economy: cities, regions and international trade. MIT Press, Cambridge
3. Batty M (2013) The new science of cities. MIT Press, Cambridge
4. Newman PW, Kenworthy JR (1989) Gasoline consumption and cities: a comparison of US cities with a global survey. J Am Plan Assoc 55:24-37
5. Bettencourt LM, Lobo L, Helbing D, Kühn C, West GB (2007) Growth, innovation, scaling, and the pace of life in cities. Proc Natl Acad Sci USA 104(17):7301-7306
6. Samaniego H, Moses ME (2008) Cities as organisms: allometric scaling of urban road networks. J Trans Land Use 1:21-39
7. Rozenfield HD, Rybski D, Andrade JS, Batty M, Stanley HE, Makse HA (2008) Laws of population growth. Proc Natl Acad Sci USA 105(48):18702-18707
8. Bettencourt LM, Lobo L, Strumsky D, West GB (2010) Urban scaling and its deviations: revealing the structure of wealth, innovation and crime across cities. PLoS ONE 5(11):13541
9. Schläpfer M, Bettencourt LM, Grauwin S, Raschke M, Claxton R, Smoreda Z, West GB, Ratti C (2014) The scaling of human interactions with city size. J R Soc Interface 11:20130789
10. Makse HA, Havlin S, Staneley HE (1995) Modelling urban growth. Nature 377:608-612
11. Bettencourt LM, West GB (2010) A unified theory of urban living. Nature 467:912-913
12. Pan W, Ghoshal G, Krumme C, Cebrian M, Pentland A (2013) Urban characteristics attributable to density-driven tie formation. Nat Commun 4:1961
13. Bettencourt LM (2013) The origin of scaling in cities. Science 340(6139):1438-1441
14. Louf R, Barthélemy M (2014) How congestion shapes cities: from mobility patterns to scaling. Sci Rep 4:5561
15. González MC, Hidalgo CA, Barabási A-L (2008) Understanding individual human mobility patterns. Nature 453(7196):779-782
16. Song C, Koren T, Wang P, Barabási A-L (2010) Modelling the scaling properties of human mobility. Nat Phys 6(10):818-823
17. Schneider CM, Belik V, Couronné T, Smoreda Z, González MC (2013) Unraveling daily human mobility motifs. J R Soc Interface 10:20130246
18. Amini A, Kung K, Kang C, Sobolevsky S, Ratti C (2014) The impact of social segregation on human mobility in developing and industrialized regions. EPJ Data Sci 3:6
19. Lu X, Bengtsson L, Holme P (2012) Predictability of population displacement after the 2010 Haiti earthquake. Proc Natl Acad Sci USA 109(29):11576-11581
20. Bengtsson L, Lu X, Garfield R, von Schreeb J (2011) Improved response to disasters and outbreaks by tracking population movements with mobile phone network data: a post-earthquake geospatial study in Haiti. PLoS Med 8:1001083
21. Wesolowski A, Eagle N, Tatem AJ, Smith DL, Noor AM, Snow RW, Buckee CO (2012) Quantifying the impact of human mobility on malaria. Science 338(6104):267-270
22. Le Menach A, Tatem AJ, Cohen JM, Hay SI, Randell H, Patil AP, Smith DL (2011) Travel risk, malaria importation and malaria transmission in Zanzibar. Sci Rep 1:93
23. Tizzoni M, Bajardi P, Decuyper A, Kon Kam King G, Schneider CM, Blondel V, Smoreda Z, Gonzalez M, Colizza V (2014) On the use of human mobility proxies for modeling epidemics. PLoS Comput Biol 10(7):1003716
24. Ratti C, Williams S, Frenchman D, Pulselli R (2006) Mobile landscapes: using location data from cell phones for urban analysis. Environ Plan B, Plan Des 33(5):727-748
25. Toole JL, Ulm M, González MC, Bauer D (2012) Inferring land use from mobile phone activity. In: Proceedings of the ACM SIGKDD international workshop on urban computing. ACM, New York, pp 1-8

26. Pei T, Sobolevsky S, Ratti C, Shaw S, Li T, Zhou C (2014) A new insight into land use classification based on aggregated mobile phone data. Int J Geogr Inf Sci 28:1-20
27. Becker RA, Caceres R, Hanson K, Loh JM, Urbanek S, Varshavsky A, Volinsky C (2011) A tale of one city: using cellular network data for urban planning. IEEE Pervasive Comput 10:18-26
28. Grauwin S, Sobolevsky S, Moritz S, Gódor I, Ratti C (2014) Towards a comparative science of cities: using mobile traffic records in New York, London and Hong Kong. arXiv:1406.4400
29. Louail T, Lenormand M, Cantu Ros OG, Picornell M, Herranz R, Frias-Martinez E, Ramasco JJ, Barthélemy M (2014) From mobile phone data to the spatial structure of cities. Sci Rep 4:5276
30. Open Data Institute Trento: Telecom Big Data Challenge. http://theodi.fbk.eu/openbigdata/
31. Wesolowski A, Eagle N, Noor AM, Snow RW, Buckee CO (2012) Heterogeneous mobile phone ownership and usage patterns in Kenya. PLoS ONE 7(4):35319
32. Comune di Milano: Milan municipality open data. http://dati.comune.milano.it/dato/item/27-27-popolazione-residente-in-anagrafe-per-cittadinanza-e-quartiere-anni-1999-2011.html
33. Eagle N, Macy M, Claxton R (2010) Network diversity and economic development. Science 328(5981):1029-1031
34. TripAdvisor: Things to do in Milan. http://www.tripadvisor.com/Attractions-g187849-Activities-Milan_Lombardy.html
35. Iglewicz B, Hoaglin D (1993) How to detect and handle outliers. The ASQC basic references in quality COntrol. Statist Techn 16
36. Jones G (2013) Three Ajax fans stabbed during fighting before Milan game. http://uk.reuters.com/article/2013/12/11/uk-soccer-champions-milan-violence-idUKBRE9BA13I20131211
37. Mocanu D, Baronchelli A, Perra N, Gonçalves B, Zhang Q, Vespignani A (2013) The twitter of babel: mapping world languages through microblogging platforms. PLoS ONE 8(4):61981
38. Edelsbrunner H, Harer J (2008) Persistent homology - a survey. Contemp Math 453:257-282
39. Carlsson G (2009) Topology and data. Bull Am Math Soc 46:255-308
40. Tausz A, Carlsson G (2011) Applications of zigzag persistence to topological data analysis. Arxiv preprint. arXiv:1108.3545
41. Yao Y, Sun J, Huang X, Bowman GR, Singh G, Lesnick M, Guibas LJ, Pande VS, Carlsson G (2009) Topological methods for exploring low-density states in biomolecular folding pathways. J Chem Phys 130(14):144115
42. Chan JM, Carlsson G, Rabadan R (2013) Topology of viral evolution. Proc Natl Acad Sci USA 110(46):18566-18571. doi:10.1073/pnas.1313480110
43. Singh G, Memoli F, Ishkhanov T, Sapiro G, Carlsson G, Ringach DL (2008) Topological analysis of population activity in visual cortex. Journal of vision 8(8):11
44. Nicolau M, Levine AJ, Carlsson G (2011) Topology based data analysis identifies a subgroup of breast cancers with a unique mutational profile and excellent survival. Proc Natl Acad Sci USA 108(17):7265-7270. doi:10.1073/pnas.1102826108
45. Lee H, Chung MK, Kang H, Kim BN, Lee DS (2011) Discriminative persistent homology of brain networks. IEEE international symposium on biomedical imaging: from nano to macro, 2011, pp 841-844
46. Singh G, Mémoli F, Carlsson GE (2007) Topological methods for the analysis of high dimensional data sets and 3D object recognition. SPBG
47. Lum PY, Singh G, Lehman A, Ishkanov T, Vejdemo-Johansson M, Alagappan M, Carlsson J, Carlsson G (2013) Extracting insights from the shape of complex data using topology. Sci Rep 3:1236
48. Silva V, Morozov D, Vejdemo-Johansson M (2011) Persistent cohomology and circular coordinates. Discrete Comput Geom 45(4):737-759
49. De Silva V, Ghrist R (2007) Coverage in sensor networks via persistent homology. Algebr Geom Topol 7:339-358
50. Horak D, Maletič S, Rajkovič M (2009) Persistent homology of complex networks. J Stat Mech 2009(03):03034
51. Petri G, Scolamiero M, Donato I, Vaccarino F (2013) Topological strata of weighted complex networks. PLoS ONE 8(6):66506
52. Personal remittances, received (% of GDP). Available at http://data.worldbank.org/indicator/BX.TRF.PWKR.DT.GD.ZS
53. Arango J (2000) Explaining migration: a critical view. Int Soc Sci J 52(165):283-296
54. Lazer D, Pentland A, Adamic LA, Aral S, Barabási A-L, Brewer D, Christakis NA, Contractor N, Fowler JH, Gutmann M, Jebara T, King G, Macy M, Roy D, Van Alstyne M (2009) Life in the network: the coming age of computational social science. Science 323(5915):721-723
55. Isaacman S, Becker R, Caceres R, Kobourov S, Martonosi M, Rowland J, Varshavsky A (2011) Identifying important places in people's lives from cellular network data. In: Lyons K, Hightower J, Huang EM (eds) Pervasive computing, 9th international conference, pervasive 2011, San Francisco, USA, June 12-15, 2011. Proceedings. Lecture notes in computer science. Springer, Berlin, pp 133-151
56. Eagle N, Pentland A, Lazer D (2009) Inferring friendship network structure by using mobile phone data. Proc Natl Acad Sci USA 106:15274-15278
57. Calabrese F, Smoreda Z, Blondel VD, Ratti C (2011) Interplay between telecommunications and face-to-face interactions: a study using mobile phone data. PLoS ONE 6(7):20814
58. Calabrese F, Colonna M, Lovisolo P, Parata D, Ratti C (2011) Real-time urban monitoring using cell phones: a case study in Rome. IEEE Trans Intell Transp Syst 1(12):141-151
59. Reades J, Calabrese F, Sevtsuk A, Ratti C (2007) Cellular census: exploration in urban data collection. IEEE Pervasive Comput 7(3):30-38
60. Reades J, Calabrese F, Ratti C (2009) Eigenplaces: analysing cities using the time-space structure of the mobile phone network. Environ Plan B, Plan Des 36:824-836
61. Palmer JRB, Espenshade TJ, Bartumeus F, Chung CY, Ozgencil NE, Li K (2013) New approaches to human mobility: using mobile phones for demographic research. Demography 50(3):1105-1128
62. Deville P, Linard C, Martin S, Gilbert M, Stevens FR, Gaughan AE, Blondel VD, Tatem AJ (2014) Dynamic population mapping using mobile phone data. Proc Natl Acad Sci USA 111(45):15888-15893
63. Smith C, Quercia D, Capra L (2013) Finger on the pulse: identifying deprivation using transit flow analysis. In: Proceedings of the 2013 conference on computer supported cooperative work. ACM, New York, pp 683-692

64. Wirz M, Franke T, Roggen D, Mitleton-Kelly E, Lukowicz P, Tröster G (2013) Probing crowd density through smartphones in city-scale mass gatherings. EPJ Data Sci 2:5

65. Massey DS (1985) Ethnic residential segregation: a theoretical synthesis and empirical review. Sociol Soc Res 69(3):315-350

66. Pamuk A (2004) Geography of immigrant clusters in global cities: a case study of San Francisco. Int J Urban Reg Res 28(2):287-307

67. Louf R, Barthelemy M (2013) Modeling the polycentric transition of cities. Phys Rev Lett 111:198702

6

The retail market as a complex system

Diego Pennacchioli[1,2], Michele Coscia[3]*, Salvatore Rinzivillo[2], Fosca Giannotti[2] and Dino Pedreschi[2,4]

*Correspondence:
michele_coscia@hks.harvard.edu
[3]CID, Harvard University, 79 JFK St,
Cambridge, USA
Full list of author information is
available at the end of the article

Abstract

Aim of this paper is to introduce the complex system perspective into retail market analysis. Currently, to understand the retail market means to search for local patterns at the micro level, involving the segmentation, separation and profiling of diverse groups of consumers. In other contexts, however, markets are modelled as complex systems. Such strategy is able to uncover emerging regularities and patterns that make markets more predictable, e.g. enabling to predict how much a country's GDP will grow. Rather than isolate actors in homogeneous groups, this strategy requires to consider the system as a whole, as the emerging pattern can be detected only as a result of the interaction between its self-organizing parts. This assumption holds also in the retail market: each customer can be seen as an independent unit maximizing its own utility function. As a consequence, the global behaviour of the retail market naturally emerges, enabling a novel description of its properties, complementary to the local pattern approach. Such task demands for a data-driven empirical framework. In this paper, we analyse a unique transaction database, recording the micro-purchases of a million customers observed for several years in the stores of a national supermarket chain. We show the emergence of the fundamental pattern of this complex system, connecting the products' volumes of sales with the customers' volumes of purchases. This pattern has a number of applications. We provide three of them. By enabling us to evaluate the sophistication of needs that a customer has and a product satisfies, this pattern has been applied to the task of uncovering the hierarchy of needs of the customers, providing a hint about what is the next product a customer could be interested in buying and predicting in which shop she is likely to go to buy it.

Keywords: marketing; complex systems; nestedness

1 Introduction

The retail market has been one among the most successful application scenarios for data mining research. Supermarkets generate a large amount of data each day, by recording which customers are buying which products, where and when. Traditional statistics tools have been abandoned, as unsuitable tools for dealing with such data richness, in favour of association rule mining [1], data clustering [2], OLAP techniques for business intelligence [3, 4] and other approaches. The common strategy shared by these tools is to segment, separate and profile diverse groups of consumers. Their typical result is to find unexpected pairwise relationships between products, or group together some customers given their purchase behaviour or personal data. We call this class of results 'local patterns', as they typically involve specific groups of customers/products, and they proved their usefulness in many real world scenarios [5–7].

There are alternative approaches to the analysis of other types of markets. In [8, 9] the global export market at the country level is modelled as a complex system. Rather than focusing on local patterns, the authors looked for a global pattern emerging from the self-organization of competing actors. Under such perspective, many fluctuating and unpredictable local behaviours can be interpreted as adjustments happening at a higher level. The world export market, then, ceases to be unpredictable and a global pattern emerges. Exploiting this new knowledge of the market as a complex system, authors are able to define the new concept of 'Economic Complexity' and prove that this measure is a very accurate predictor of a country's future growth, outperforming any other traditional socio-economical indicator. This approach is very successful and it has been replicated elsewhere [10].

In this paper, we introduce the idea of analysing the retail market as a complex system. Our approach is based on the observation that the retail market is composed by independent units, the customers, which act accordingly to their internal logic, the maximization of their utility function. By putting together these interacting units, the system of retail market starts showing properties of its own, as a result of the self organization of the customers. This approach has the potential to overcome some severe limitations of the classical retail market data mining. For instance, the output of association rule mining is usually composed by thousands rules, each describing a single particle of the customer behaviour, and selecting the most representative ones is usually a problem [11]. Moreover, usually many products are not present in the result set, as they are not frequently purchased, causing this description to be incomplete. On the downside, we forfeit the high granularity and precision achievable with data mining techniques.

By looking at the retail market as a complex system, we are able to define the Purchase Function, which is a description of the mechanics of this complex system at the global level. The Purchase Function enables us to enhance our knowledge about the system as a whole, describing both customers and products, and we prove its usefulness in three different analyses. First, we provide one empirical observation of Maslow's hierarchy of needs [12]. Using the Purchase Function we discover that highly ranked customers, with more sophisticated needs, tend to buy niche products, i.e., low-ranked products; on the other hand, low-ranked, low purchase volume customers tend buy only high-ranked product, very popular products that everyone buys.

Second, we propose a simple marketing application useful for targeted advertising. Given that the Purchase Function classifies the likelihood of a customer-product connection, a target marketing campaign may spot with a higher accuracy the smallest customer set that is likely to start buying a given product.

Finally, our third application is focused on the predictability of customer movements on the territory. We aim at predicting in which shop a customer will go to buy a given product. We show how the typical low-level information about the product (its price or its usual purchase amounts) have some explanatory power. However, our customer/product sophistication measure, derived from the Purchase Function, has a much greater explanatory power.

Our applications are founded on a data-driven empirical proof. We analyse a unique transaction database, collected by a retail supermarket chain in Italy, which recorded the micro-purchases of a million customers. Each customer is recognizable as the system

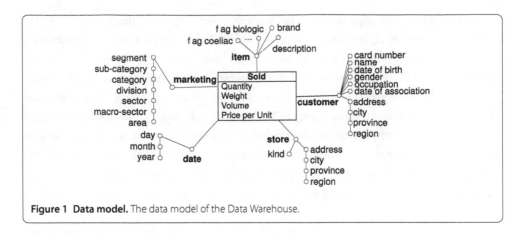

Figure 1 Data model. The data model of the Data Warehouse.

records her purchases using the identification code of her membership card. We are then able to track the purchases of each customers over a four year period, from 2007 to 2011.

In our analysis, we build the adjacency matrix of the bipartite network connecting a customer to the products she buys. This matrix has a triangular shape, consistent with the observations of the global export market [8, 9]. We prove that this shape is not expected, by implementing a simple null model of customer behaviour and observing that the fundamental properties of the observed matrix structure are not present in the null model matrix. Therefore, the observed system is indeed the product of a complex interaction not reducible to simple assumptions. We then proceed to define the Purchase Function, which divides the adjacency matrix in expressed and not expressed connections. This is the global pattern of the system and we can exploit it in our application scenarios.

2 The data

Our analysis is based on real world data about customer behaviour. The dataset we used is the retail market data of one of the largest Italian retail distribution companies. The conceptual data model of the data warehouse is depicted in Figure 1. The whole dataset contains retail market data in a time window that goes from January 1st, 2007 to December 31st, 2011. The active and recognizable customers are 1,066,020. A customer is active if she has purchased something during the data time window, while she is recognizable if the purchase has been made using a membership card. The customers of this supermarket with a card are very engaged in the shop itself: the supermarket is in fact a cooperative and whoever has the card is considered a member. This makes the data more valuable as the customers with a card have very high incentives to buy whatever they can in this supermarket, making it the primary (and sometimes only) source of the products they buy. In fact, a study by Bocconi showed that COOP is able to score among the highest in the metrics of customer fidelity.[a] The 138 stores of the company cover the whole west coast of Italy, selling 345,208 different items.

An important dimension of the data warehouse is Marketing, representing the classification of products: it is organized as a tree and it represents a hierarchy built on the product typologies, designed by marketing experts of the company. The top level of this hierarchy is called 'Area' that split the products into two fundamental categories: 'Food' and 'No Food'. The bottom level of the hierarchy, the one that contains the leaves of the tree, is called 'Segment' and it contains 7,003 different values. Hence, for each item contained in the dataset, there is an entry assigning it to the right path of the hierarchy tree.

Table 1 Distribution of the number of products per category

Food	2,026 (77.6%)	Fresh	1,005 (70.9%)	Regular	493 (78.8%)
				Very fresh	512 (63.2%)
		Various	1,021 (84.1%)	Chemicals	333 (83.4%)
				Grocery	688 (84.5%)
No food	2,791 (37.8%)	-	2,791 (37.8%)	House	565 (54.9%)
				Multimedia	368 (33.5%)
				Personal	746 (32.0%)
				Seasonal & DIY	1,112 (34.4%)

In parenthesis, we report the percentage of the products that are sold in all three types of shops in our dataset.

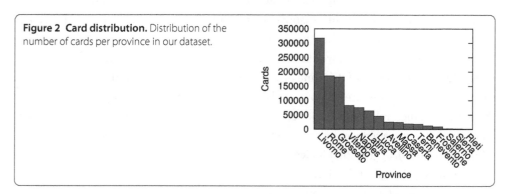

Figure 2 Card distribution. Distribution of the number of cards per province in our dataset.

The 'Store Kind' column refers to the shop classification: in increasing order of size we have 'Gestin', 'Super' and 'Iper'. 'Gestin' are usually low area shops, occupying the ground floor of a building, usually in the city center and in smaller towns and villages. 'Super' are larger, usually occupying their own building and built into larger cities just outside the city center. 'Iper' are usually an Italian equivalent of US malls.

In Table 1 we report how many segments are allocated in the top three levels of the marketing classification, proving that the supermarket is indeed selling a complete variety of products, not just grocery and fresh food. We also report the percentage of products that are sold at all three types of shops. While it is expected that the share of non-food products sold in smaller shops is lower, gestin shops still sell a significant quantity of them.[b] For example, the absolute number of DIY products sold in the smallest shops is practically equivalent to the absolute number of fresh food products.

Given that the dataset contains more than one million customers and almost 350k items, to build a matrix 'customers × items' would generate a ∼370 billion cells matrix, that is redundant for our purposes. Hence we need to reduce both dimensions (customers and items). There are two main criteria to select the customers: on the basis of their purchase behaviour (e.g. excluding from the analysis all the people that did not purchased at least a total number x items) or geographically (e.g. considering just the customers of an area). We decided to apply the latter filter, since we do not want to exclude any customer behaviour apriori. We select a subset of shops in the dataset belonging to the same areas of Italy. The number of cards per area is presented in Figure 2. Note that there might be some double-counting due to lost cards. However, this should not influence the analysis because customer behavior is constant regardless if she lost her card or not and, being our observations cumulative and normalized as explained in later sections, this double counting is bounded to have limited effect only in the fitted parameters, not in the overall phenomenon.

We generated different views of the dataset for different purposes. Our main dataset is Livorno2007-2009, that is including all the purchases of the customers located in the city of Livorno during the period from 2007 to 2009. We use only this view for the applications of the framework's output. We also generated the dataset Lazio2007-2009 (same period, different geographical location, the union of the cities of Rome, Viterbo, Latina, Rieti and Frosinone) and Livorno2010-2011 (different period, same geographical location). The two views are generated to prove that the fundamental properties of the adjacency matrix needed for our framework are not bounded to a particular place or time. The following steps of data preparation are applied equally to the different datasets extracted.

The second issue, as introduced above, regards the cardinality of products. There is a conceptual problem in using the level of detail of 'item': the granularity is too fine, making the analysis impractical as it would consider a very low detail level. The distinction between different packages of the same product, e.g. different sizes of bottles containing the same liquid, is not of interest in our study. A natural way to solve this problem is to use the marketing hierarchy of the products, substituting the item with its marketing Segment value. In this way, we reduce the cardinality of the dimension of the product by 98% (from 345,208 to 7,003), aggregating logically equivalent products.

The last step in data selection is to exclude from the analysis all segments that are either too frequent (e.g. the shopping bag) or meaningless for the purchasing analysis (e.g. discount vouchers, errors, segments never sold, etc.). After this last filter, and consequently the discharge of the customers that bought exclusively products classified under the removed segments, we got the adjacency matrix, the input to our framework. Livorno2007-2009 matrix has 317,269 customers and 4,817 segments, with 182,821,943 purchases; Livorno2010-2011 has 326,010 customers and 4,807 segments, with 183,679,550 purchases; and Lazio2007-2009 has 278,154 customers and 4,641 segments, with 135,517,300 purchases.

3 Methods

Analysing customers' purchase behaviour is one of major success stories of data mining research. The pioneer work on association rules [1] is still one of most cited papers in computer science. However, we believe that data mining is able to take into account only a part of the whole picture, not accounting for a great amount of valuable data. Firstly, it excludes customers, that are used only for counting the support of products. Secondly, as many natural phenomena, purchasing behaviour is characterized by long tail distributions. In Figures 3 and 4 we depict the cumulative frequency for products and customers

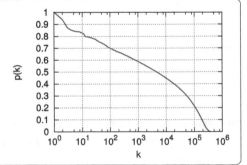

Figure 3 Cumulative product frequency distribution. The cumulative frequency distribution ($p(k)$) of products in a transactional dataset. By frequency (k) we mean the number of times a products has been put in a shopping cart. It is a concept equivalent to the support, used in the association rule mining literature.

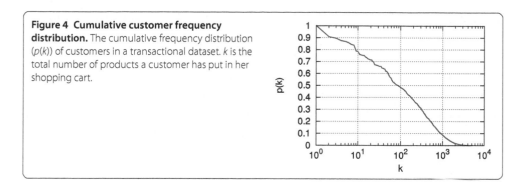

Figure 4 Cumulative customer frequency distribution. The cumulative frequency distribution ($p(k)$) of customers in a transactional dataset. k is the total number of products a customer has put in her shopping cart.

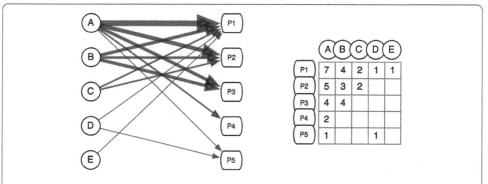

Figure 5 The bipartite purchase graph. A representation of the bipartite purchase graph, connecting customers to the product they buy. On the right, the purchase graph is represented as an adjacency matrix.

in a transactional dataset. The plots describe the probability (y axis) of a product (customer) being bought by (buying) at least a given number of customers (products). The distributions are skewed with a long tail, spanning several orders of magnitude, with 20% products bought only by at less than 10 customers, and 20% customers buying less than 10 products. As a consequence, a large amount of products is not considered in association rule mining, as these products fail to meet the frequency threshold. Moreover, the connections between the most popular products are not randomly distributed into the dataset, as they tend to be connected to the same set of customers, the ones buying everything. So, in association rule mining we only consider the products that are being bought by the same set of big buyers, ignoring all the other customer classes. A methodology able to include customers and less popular products into a global picture can be useful as a complementary part of association rule mining.

This is what we aim to do by looking at the entire transactional dataset as a complex system. Our proposal can be summarized by representing the purchases of customers and products as a weighted bipartite graph $G = (C, P, E)$, connecting a customer $c_i \in C$ to a product $p_j \in P$ she bought. The weight w on the edge $(c_i, p_j, w) \in E$ is the number of times customer c_i bought product p_j. A depiction of our model is provided in Figure 5. Our methodology aims at returning two different descriptions of the complex system of retail: the global and the local descriptors of the bipartite structure. At the global level, we generate the Purchase Function (f_*) connecting the volume of sales of products with the set of customers buying them and the volume of purchases of customers with the set of products they are buying. At the local level we perform an evaluation of how much a product, and a customer's need, is basic or sophisticated. We call it Product (and Customer) Sophistication.

The methodology is implemented in a three-step process: (i) pre-process, where the data about customer purchases is transformed in a format suitable for our analysis; (ii) analysis, where we calculate the Purchase Function and the Product/Customer Sophistication; (iii) validation, where through a null model we evaluate the significance of the descriptors. We now proceed describing these three steps, starting from the pre-process.

3.1 Pre-process

The first step of our methodology is to pre process the connections between customers and products. This operation is carried on the adjacency matrix of the bipartite network customer-product. We are interested in showing that the best sold products are bought by all customers, while products with a low market share are bought exclusively by customers who buy everything. To highlight this pattern, we sort the matrix with the following criterion: fixing the top-left corner of the matrix M as the origin, we sort the customers on the basis of the sum of the items purchased in descending order (the top buying customer at the first row and so on), and the products with the same criteria from left to right (the best seller product at the first column and so on). In this way, at the cell $(0,0)$ we find the quantity of best seller product purchased by the top buying customer.

The final step of data preparation is to binarize the matrix, by identifying which purchases are significant and which are not. We cannot simply binarize the matrix considering the purchase presence/absence of a customer for a product. A matrix with a 1 if the customer c_j purchased the product p_i and 0 otherwise will result in a certain amount of noise: it takes only a single purchase to connect a customer to a product, even if generally the customer buys large amounts of everything else and the product is generally purchased in larger amount by every other customer.

We evaluate the meaningfulness of a purchase quantity, for each product p_i for each customer c_j, by calculating its Revealed Comparative Advantage (RCA), following [8]. Given a product p_i and a customer c_j, the RCA of the couple is defined as follows:

$$\text{RCA}(p_i, c_j) = \frac{X(p_i, c_j)}{X(p_*, c_j)} \left(\frac{X(p_i, c_*)}{X(p_*, c_*)} \right)^{-1},$$

where $X(p_i, c_j)$ is the number of p_i bought by c_j, $X(p_*, c_j)$ is the total number of products bought by c_j, $X(p_i, c_*)$ is the total number of times p_i has been sold and $X(p_*, c_*)$ is the total number of products sold.

RCA takes values from 0 (when $X(p_i, c_j) = 0$, i.e. customer c_j never bought a single instance of product p_i) to $+\infty$. When $\text{RCA}(p_i, c_j) = 1$, it means that $X(p_i, c_j)$ is exactly the expected value under the assumption of statistical independence, i.e. the connection between customer c_j and product p_i has the expected weight. If $\text{RCA}(p_i, c_j) < 1$ it means that the customer c_j purchased the product p_i less than expected, and vice versa. Therefore, the value of 1 for the RCA indicator is a reasonable threshold to discern the meaningfulness of the quantity purchased: if it is strictly higher, then the purchases are meaningful and the corresponding cell in the binary matrix is 1; otherwise the purchases are not meaningful, even if some purchases are actually made, and the corresponding cell in the binary matrix

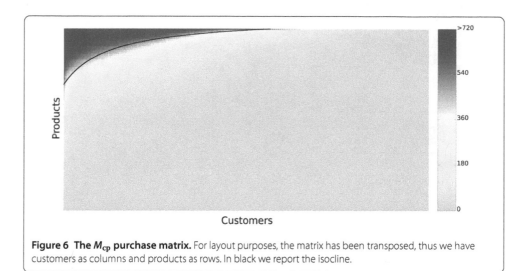

Figure 6 The M_{cp} purchase matrix. For layout purposes, the matrix has been transposed, thus we have customers as columns and products as rows. In black we report the isocline.

is 0. The M_{cp} matrix is built accordingly to this rule:

$$M_{cp} = \begin{cases} 1 & \text{if } \text{RCA}(p_i, c_j) > 1; \\ 0 & \text{otherwise.} \end{cases}$$

This is the final output of the preprocess phase, hence from now on it will be referred as the purchase matrix M_{cp}, and $M_{cp}(c_j, p_i)$ is the entry of M_{cp} of row j and column i.

The M_{cp} purchase matrix for the Livorno2007-2009 dataset, result of the pre-process phase, is depicted in Figure 6. In Figure 6, the columns of the matrix are the 317,269 customers and the rows are the 4,817 products. We depicted a compressed view of the matrix, where each data dot represent a 50×50 square of the original matrix and the gradient represents how many 1's are present in that section of the matrix, for space constraints.

We can observe in Figure 6 the phenomenon we expect given our assumptions: only a small amount of popular products are bought by everyone, but smaller sets of customers purchase the rest of the products (going from the right to the left columns). The same set of big buyers are always part of these smaller and smaller sets.

Livorno2010-2011 and Lazio2007-2009 matrices are depicted in Figures 7 and 8, left and right respectively (the legend for both figures is the same as Figure 6 legend). From Figures 7 and 8 we can see that the triangularity of the M_{cp} matrix is constant, regardless the geographical and/or temporal selection of the data.

3.2 Analysis

In this phase, the aim is to obtain the global and local descriptors of the complex system of retail. For the global level, we define the function f_* connecting the volume of sales of products with the set of customers buying them and the volume of purchases of customers with the set of products they are buying. At the local level we perform an evaluation of how much a product, and a customer's need, is basic or sophisticated. We start with the global level and then we proceed describing the local level.

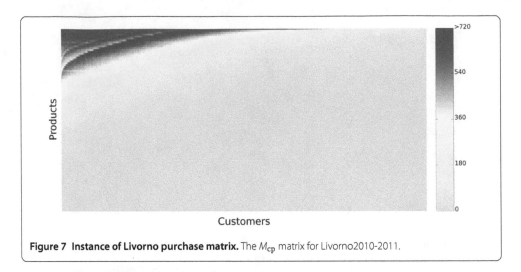

Figure 7 Instance of Livorno purchase matrix. The M_{cp} matrix for Livorno2010-2011.

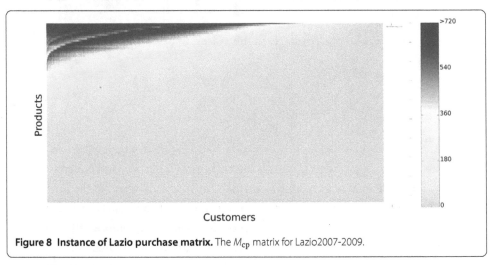

Figure 8 Instance of Lazio purchase matrix. The M_{cp} matrix for Lazio2007-2009.

3.2.1 Global descriptor

Customer behaviour is not random: as we have seen there are many studies dealing with the problem of finding correlations between products frequently bought together [1]. However, here we strengthen this assumption as follows: these correlations are actually organized following a general function that regulates retail purchases. In other words, we are not dealing with a set of correlations limiting their effects on two or three products. There exists a general pattern, meaning that it is possible to define the set of products bought by a customer as a function of the amount of products she buys. We call this the Purchase Function.

The Purchase Function states that the assortment of products bought by any given customer c_j is determined by c_j's volume of purchase, and the population of customers that buy any given product p_i is determined by p_i's volume of sales. More precisely, we indicate it as a f_* function, that relates the *rank* of products with the *rank* of customers, where the rank i of a product p_i (or j for customer c_j) stands for the fact that p_i is the ith highest sold product (or c_j is the jth customer with the largest volume of purchases). In practice, looking at the $M_{c,p}$ matrix in Figure 6, the f_* function is the equation of the line dividing the area with the high density of ones (colored in red) from the rest.

For any customer c_j we denote assortment(c_j) = $\{p_1,\ldots,p_{f_*(j)}\}$ and, for any product p_i, customer_base(p_i) = $\{c_1,\ldots,c_{f_*^{-1}(i)}\}$. The Purchase Function is assumed to be a decreasing monotonic function, i.e., $i_1 < i_2$ implies that $f_*(i_1) > f_*(i_2)$, which in turn implies that assortment(c_2) $\subseteq$ assortment(c_1). In other words, if c_1 is a customer purchasing more in terms of product quantities than c_2, then it is very likely that c_1 buys the same set of products c_2 buys, plus something more.

Matrices with triangular structures have been already studied in ecology literature. In ecosystems, simpler organisms are ubiquitous and more complex organisms appear *iff* simpler organisms are already present [13]. In these works, authors define nestedness as a measure to understand how much triangular is the structure of the matrix representing the connections between species and ecosystems. The nestedness is calculated by identifying the border dividing the matrix in two areas containing respectively most ones and most zeroes, that is exactly the role of the Purchase Function. In this literature, this is known as *isocline*.

In literature there are several algorithms tackling the problem of computing the isocline of a matrix [14]. The general approach is usually made in two steps: a reordering of the rows and columns of the matrix, such that the ones tend to be clustered in the upper-left corner of the matrix; and an estimate of the isocline function on the reordered matrix.

In our framework we are implementing an alternative way to calculate the Purchase Function (isocline). We have chosen to do so for two reasons. First, all algorithms explicitly reorder the matrix. We do not want to reorder our matrix, since the order we defined in the pre-process is a fundamental prerequisite for the purchase function, as it has been defined above to connect the ranks of customers and products calculated on their volumes of purchases and sales, respectively. These ranks are obtained by the matrix ordering during the preprocessing stage and thus this order cannot be modified. Secondly, the state-of-the-art algorithms are designed to deal with ecology data, with a number of cells in the order of 10^4 or 10^5. Since our cells are $\sim 10^9$, we need to define a new procedure, enabling the application of our framework to large datasets. We described the specifications of this methodology in a previously published technical report [15].

We need an evaluation measure to understand if a proposed isocline is good or not. We use the following formulation:

$$N(M_{\mathrm{cp}},f_*) = \frac{1}{2}\left(\frac{f_l(M_{\mathrm{cp}},1)}{f_l(M_{\mathrm{cp}},*)} + \frac{f_r(M_{\mathrm{cp}},0)}{f_r(M_{\mathrm{cp}},*)}\right),$$

where $f_l(M_{\mathrm{cp}},*)$ counts the number of cells at the left of the isocline in M_{cp} where we expect to find the ones (and $f_l(M_{\mathrm{cp}},1)$ counts the ones) and where $f_r(M_{\mathrm{cp}},*)$ counts the number of cells at the right of the isocline in M_{cp} where we expect to find the zeroes (and $f_r(M_{\mathrm{cp}},0)$ counts the zeroes). In practice, we take the average of the one-density at the left and zero-density at the right of the isocline. We used this measure because simply counting unexpected presences and absences of ones at the right/left of the isocline is not a fair measure, being our matrix very sparse.

We now need to find the isocline. To find it, we estimate where the isocline should pass to maximize the division of ones at the left and zeroes at the right. We consider our matrix as a Cartesian space. For each discrete x axis value (customer) we get an estimate of where the isocline should pass (y axis). We do so by summing the ones of the corresponding matrix row ($k_{c,0} = \sum_p M_{\mathrm{cp}}(c,p)$). Then, for each discrete y axis value (product) we get

Table 2 The $N(M_{cp}, f_*)$ for the different f_* shapes tested

f_*	$N(M_{cp}, f_*)$
$ax + b$	0.616106811666
$ax^2 + bx + c$	0.628533747603
$a\log(x) + b$	0.623911138356
ax^b	0.572996769269
$\frac{a}{x}$	0.609588181022
$-\frac{ax+b}{cx+d}$	0.632547410976

Table 3 The $N(M_{cp}, f_*)$ for the different views of the dataset

M_{cp}	$N(M_{cp}, f_*)$
Livorno2007-2009	0.632547410976
Lazio2007-2009	0.622983174602
Livorno2010-2011	0.615276275848
Null model average	0.5892564877

an estimate of where the isocline should pass (x axis). We do so by summing the ones of the corresponding matrix column ($k_{0,p} = \sum_c M_{cp}(c,p)$). We average these two values and we obtain a pair of coordinates. This procedure is linear in the number of customers and products and therefore it can scale with very big matrices. We fit these coordinates using a non-linear least squares optimization with the Levenberg-Marquardt algorithm [16] to obtain the best function able to represent the isocline and, therefore, the Purchase Function.

To fit a function with the non-linear least squares optimization, the shape of the function is needed. Our framework tries several different shapes, storing the corresponding $N(M_{cp}, f_*)$ value and then choosing the best performing one. In our case, we obtained a simple hyperbola in all the three cases in exam. The $N(M_{cp}, f_*)$ results of different f_* formulations for the Livorno2007-2009 matrix are reported in Table 2. The evaluation via the $N(M_{cp}, f_*)$ function of the goodness of the division operated by the isocline for all datasets and the null model is provided in Table 3. The null model average reported in the last row of Table 3 has been calculated averaging 30 iterations. As we can see, the average value for null model is lower. Its standard deviation is in the order of 10^{-5}. Therefore, we can conclude that the difference is also significant.

For the Livorno2007-2009 dataset, the value of the f_* parameters has been estimated as: $\alpha = 11{,}318.559$, $\beta = 94.2526$, $\gamma = 0.2834$, $\delta = -16{,}866{,}558$. The corresponding isocline has been plotted in black in Figure 6. We do not report the values of the parameters for the other datasets as we are not using them in the rest of the paper.

3.2.2 Local descriptor

As for the local descriptor, we quantify the sophistication level of the products sold and of the needs of the customers buying products. The basic intuition is that more sophisticated products are by definition less needed, as they are expression of a more complex need. One may be tempted to answer to this question by trivially returning the products in descending order of their popularity: the more a product is sold, the more basic it is. However, this is not considering an important aspect of the problem: to be sold to a large set of costumers is a condition to be considered 'basic', but it does not fully describe the term. Another condition is that the set of customers buying the product should include the set of costumers with the lowest level of sophistication of their needs. The conjunction of the two properties is closer to define a product as 'basic'.

This conjunction is not trivial and it is made possible by the triangular structure of the adjacency matrix. Consider Figure 6: the columns in the right part of the matrix are those customers buying only few products. Those products are more or less bought by everyone. In a world where our theory does not hold, instead of buying the products at the top row of the matrix they would buy random products.

For this reason, we need to evaluate at the same time the level of sophistication of a product and of the needs of a customer using the data in the purchase matrix, and recursively correct the one with the other. We adapt the procedure of [17], adjusting it for our big data.

We calculated the sums of the purchase matrix for each customer ($k_{c,0} = \sum_p M_{cp}(c,p)$) and product ($k_{0,p} = \sum_c M_{cp}(c,p)$) to estimate the isocline for the Purchase Function f_*. To generate a more accurate measure of the sophistication of a product we need to correct the sums recursively: this requires us to calculate the average level of sophistication of the customers' needs by looking at the average sophistication of the products that they buy, and then use it to update the average sophistication of these products, and so forth. This can be expressed as follows: $k_{N,p} = \frac{1}{k_{0,p}} \sum_c M_{cp} k_{c,N-1}$. We then insert $k_{c,N-1}$ into $k_{N,p}$ obtaining:

$$k_{N,p} = \frac{1}{k_{0,p}} \sum_c M_{cp} \frac{1}{k_{c,0}} \sum_{p'} M_{cp'} k_{N-2,p'},$$

$$k_{N,p} = \sum_{p'} k_{N-2,p'} \sum_c \frac{M_{cp} M_{cp'}}{k_{0,p} k_{c,0}}$$

and rewrite this as:

$$k_{N,p} = \sum_{p'} \widetilde{M}_{pp'} k_{N-2,p'},$$

where:

$$\widetilde{M}_{pp'} = \sum_c \frac{M_{cp} M_{cp'}}{k_{0,p} k_{c,0}}.$$

We note in the last formulation $k_{N,p}$ is satisfied when $k_{N,p} = k_{N-2,p}$ and this is equal to a certain constant a. This is the eigenvector which is associated with the largest eigenvalue (that is equal to one).[c] Since this eigenvector is a vector composed by the same constant, it is not informative. We look, instead, for the eigenvector associated with the second largest eigenvalue. This is the eigenvector associated with the variance in the system and thus it is the correct estimate of product sophistication.

However, this formulation is very sensitive to noise, i.e. products that are bought only by a very narrow set of customers. To calculate the eigenvector on the entire set of products generates a small amount of products whose sophistication level is seven orders of magnitude larger than the rest of the products. This variance provokes the other sophistication estimates to be flattened down to the same values and therefore not meaningful. However, we do not want to simply cut the least sold products, as we aim to create a full product hierarchy, including the least sold products. To normalize this, we employ a three step strategy. First, we calculate the eigenvector on a restricted number of more popular products, purchased by at least a given threshold δ of customers. Then we use the estimate of the sophistication of these products to estimate the sophistication of the entire set of customers (that is, as defined before, the average sophistication of the restricted set of products they buy). Finally, we use the estimated sophistication of the customers to have the final sophistication of the entire set of products, again by averaging the sophistication of the customers buying them. Hence, we define the product sophistication index (PS) as:

$$PS = -\frac{\vec{K} - \mu(\vec{K})}{\sigma(\vec{K})},$$

where $\vec{K}$ is the eigenvector of $\widetilde{M}_{pp'}$ associated to the second largest eigenvalue, normalized as described above; $\mu(\vec{K})$ is its average and $\sigma(\vec{K})$ its standard deviation. The Customer Sophistication CS is calculated using the very same procedure, by estimating $k_{c,N}$ instead of $k_{N,p}$.

Notice that there are alternatives for the computation of the sophistication measure. One among the most popular is [18], where the product complexity is formulated in terms of 'country fitness'. Instead of defining product complexity as the sum of the complexities of the countries producing the product, the authors of [18] use the inverse of the sum of the inverse complexities:

$$k_{N,p} = \frac{1}{\sum_c M_{c,p} \frac{1}{k_{c,N-1}}}.$$

The aim is to maximize the impact of countries with low complexity in dragging down the complexity of the products made mostly by them. There are upsides and downsides to each measuring choices, and this case is not different. However, the measure proposed in [18] is highly correlated with our choice, as shown in [19]. Therefore, in the context of this paper, there is no reason to prefer one measure over the other, and we make the choice of using only one for clarity and readability.

As example of the Product and Customer Sophistication calculation, we report the most and least sophisticated products for the Livorno2007-2009 dataset. We do not report the Customer Sophistication for privacy concerns. In Table 4 we report a selection of the least sophisticated products, i.e. the ones with the lowest PS values, in the purchase matrix. The less sophisticated products should be intuitively the ones covering the most basic human needs, and this intuition is confirmed by the reported products: bread, water, fruits and milk. On the other hand, Table 5 reports the most sophisticated products, i.e. the ones with the largest PS values, that intuitively should be products satisfying high-level non-necessary, probably luxury, needs. In fact, what we find in Table 5 are hi-tech products (LCD televisions, DVD compilations, computer accessories), jewellery and very specific clothing. Note that these results only apply to the particular time and location studied here. Different cultures and different countries with different economic levels can only be described by collecting appropriate additional data.

3.3 Validation

The triangular structure of the matrix in Figure 6 gives an important information: a customer that purchased few products is expected to have bought just products that are best

Table 4 A selection of the more basic products according to their *PS* values

p_i	*PS*
Regular bread	−4.41
Natural still water	−4.19
Yellow nectarines (peaches)	−3.84
Semi-skimmed fresh milk	−3.81
Bananas	−3.53

Table 5 A selection of the more sophisticated products according to their *PS* values

p_i	*PS*
LCD 28"/30" televisions	2.91
DVD music compilations	2.86
Sauna clothing	2.66
Jewelry bracelets	2.53
RAM memories	2.33

sellers. This disagrees with the expected presence of 'cherry pickers', i.e. customers that are particularly sensible and responsive to sales, especially if the sales are placed on expensive goods. Instead, looking at Figure 6, we expect customers to follow a general pattern.

Starting from this consideration, we need to validate the model, in particular we want to control that the triangular structure is meaningful. We need a null model definition with which to compare our theory. We identify three important features that our null model must hold: (1) the purchases are distributed randomly; (2) customers must preserve the total amount of their purchases; and (3) each product must preserve its sale volume on the market. The implementation of the null model is reported in the Appendix.

We depict the null matrix for Livorno2007-2009 in Figure 9, that is an accurate depiction also of the typical null matrix for Livorno2010-2011 and Lazio2007-2009. We can see that Figure 9 still presents some of the characteristic of the original M_{cp} matrix. However, in Figure 9 popular customers/products tend to have randomly distributed RCAs (therefore their columns/rows appear white in the compressed view) and, while preserving some triangularity, the null model matrix have a tendency to display more ones on the main diagonal than the original M_{cp} matrix. We can conclude that the null hypothesis, i.e. the

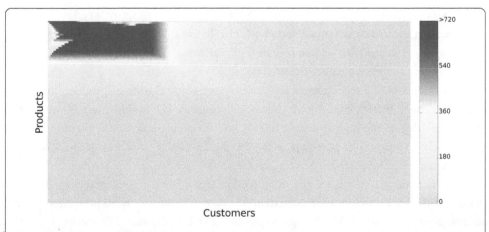

Figure 9 One instance of the null purchase matrix. To be consistent with Figure 6, also the null matrix has been transposed.

simple distribution of volume of sales and of purchases of products/customers, explain only part of the observed structure, but the original M_{cp} matrix presents some characteristics that cannot be generated randomly just by the distributions of volume of sales for the products and volume of purchases for the customers.

4 Results

In the previous section we have defined our methodology to extract the general pattern governing customer behaviour, by analysing the adjacency matrix of the bipartite structure connecting the customers to the products they are buying. In this section, we apply our methodology to real world data. We firstly describe the nature of our data. We then move on to describe the data selection policy. Then, we apply the framework, obtaining the global descriptor in the form of the Purchase Function, and the local descriptor, i.e. the sophistication levels of customers and products. Finally, we provide our three analyses: the empirical observation of Maslow's hierarchy of needs [12]; the marketing application for targeted advertising; and finally the evaluation of predictability of customer movements on the territory.

4.1 Data-driven hierarchy of needs

In this section we want to use the information provided by the Product Sophistication index to reconstruct the hierarchy of needs of the supermarket customers, and therefore provide an empirical observation of the theory of Maslow [12].

Three caveats need to be specified. First: we are not claiming that this hierarchy of needs is universal. The result we are presenting in this paper has been reached with data from one city of Italy (Livorno) and therefore it describes the hierarchy of needs of that particular city. However we showed that the triangular structure of the purchase matrix is present even in different areas of Italy (Figures 7 and 8) and therefore our framework could be applied to different world regions, helping to create a picture of different hierarchies of needs. The comparison of hierarchies of needs of different cities and the evaluation of different cultural perspectives of customers over their needs is left as future development. Further, this hierarchy is a valuable marketing tool for that particular city: products at the basis of the hierarchy are more needed, thus no marketing strategies are required for them as they will be sold anyway.

The second caveat is that we built the hierarchy of needs using the product category classification defined by the supermarket owners. To use this classification introduces the bias of a set of people, with a given culture and marketing aims. We plan to use for future developments standard product classifications.

Lastly, a collection of customers could be buying some classes of products in different shops, thus unfairly pushing up their sophistication. While this effect is considered to be small due to the high customer fidelity and the all around service provided by the supermarket, some of the products at the top of our hierarchy of needs could be over-represented.

With this caution in mind, we now build the hierarchy. To build the hierarchy we need to divide products in classes according to their PS value. Formally, we need to segment the PS values, previously sorted. We decided to perform a one-dimensional clustering using the ck-means algorithm. ck-means is an evolution of the k-means algorithm which guarantees the optimality of clustering [20]. The k-means problem is to partition data into k groups

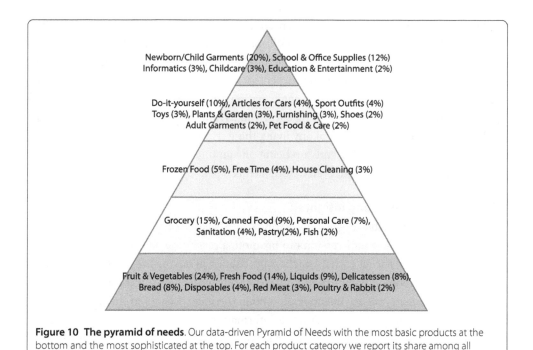

Figure 10 The pyramid of needs. Our data-driven Pyramid of Needs with the most basic products at the bottom and the most sophisticated at the top. For each product category we report its share among all purchases at that level of the hierarchy.

such that the sum of squared Euclidean distances to each group mean is minimized. ck-means is optimized to operate on one dimensional data, which is our application setting. In this setting ck-means find the optimal cluster separation, which is unique and therefore a repeatable result, properties that standard k-means does not hold.

We set $k = 5$, as we follow Maslow's hierarchy of needs classification [12] and we want to obtain roughly the following classes of products: fundamental for survival, basic needs, complementary needs, accessory needs and luxury needs. The results of the ck-means clustering have been depicted in Figure 10. In Figure 10 for each level of the hierarchy we report its main composition according to the product categories. The share values between the parenthesis tell, given the total amount of products purchases at that level of the hierarchy, how many of those belong to that particular category. For instance, skimmed and semi-skimmed milk may belong to two different hierarchy levels, say 0 and 1, and they have respectively been sold 4,000 and 2,000 times. Let us say that the total amount of products sold in hierarchy levels 0 and 1 are respectively 4,000,000 and 1,500,000. Then, skimmed milk contributes to level 0 as 0.1%, while semi-skimmed milk contributes to level 1 as 0.13%. We report only categories representing at least 2% of the hierarchy level. We did not report the single product segment, as they are too specific and too many: for instance apples, pears, bananas, tomatoes, potatoes and so on have been aggregate in the product category 'Fruits & Vegetables'. Of course, products in the same category may fall in different hierarchy levels: in Figure 10 we chose to put the category where it occupies the largest share of the level purchases.

Figure 10 is clear depiction of what are the priorities in the mind of the customers of Livorno. Figure 10 is telling some expected and some unexpected things. First there are the basic needs: drinking and eating, particularly fruit, vegetables, bread and meat. Then, there are more sophisticated eating products and what is needed to take care of the body hygiene. At the middle of the hierarchy we start to have product not strictly necessary for survival: house cleaning and simple products for the free time. The two most sophisticated needs are schooling, entertainment (both for children and adults), more complex garnishment; and, climbing at the top of the pyramid, newborn childcare and unnecessary equipment. The basis of the pyramid is expected: most basic needs are food and personal hygiene. Up until now we have basic confirmation about human needs. The top of the pyramid is instead telling us something surprising. Traditionally, reproduction is considered one of the most basic needs of any living thing. However, what we see is that in our modern society to have a baby ends up being one among the most sophisticated needs, and the first one to be dropped, even before having a pet.

4.2 Data-driven marketing insights

We now describe a possible targeted marketing strategy based on the outputs of our framework. Suppose the supermarket wants to promote a product p_i and it wants to limit its target to the smallest subset with the highest probability of buying the product advertised. The Purchase Function f_* can be used in the following way: given the amount of products bought by customer c_j we use its index j to obtain the index $f_*(j) = i$ of the most sophisticated product p_i that c_j is buying. With this information, we can derive the set of products she is expected to buy, that is assortment(c_j). assortment(c_j) is defined as all the products that have an index $i' \leq i$. The same applies considering as input a product p_i, we obtain the index delimiting the set of customers buying it (for which $j' \leq f_*^{-1}(i)$).

One concern needs to be addressed before continuing: how well is the Purchase Function dividing the ones from the zeros in comparison to what we expect? How much is a customer more likely to buy a product following the Purchase Function evaluated on our real world data (P_f) over any random product (P)?

As previously reported, the Livorno2007-2009 $M_{c,p}$ matrix contains ~37 millions ones out of ~1.5 billions cells. This means that, given a random product p_i and a random customer c_j, the baseline probability $P(p_i, c_j)$ that customer c_j is buying product p_i in a significant amount (i.e. RCA(c_j, p_i) > 1) is the ratio of these two numbers, or $P(p_i, c_j) = 2.44\%$. If we consider only the portion of the matrix at the left of the calculated isocline, i.e. the area of the matrix for which f_* tells us that the customers are very likely to buy exactly that products, we count 16,748,048 ones and 60,025,000 total cells. Thus, the probability $P_f(p_i, c_j)$ for a customer c_j to buy significant amounts of a product p_i for which $i \leq -\frac{\alpha j + \delta}{\gamma j + \beta}$ (i.e. $p_i \in$ assortment(c_j)) is 27.9%. Using the Purchase Function f_*, we can narrow of two orders of magnitude the set of combinations of products and customers to analyse and still capturing almost half of the significant purchases. In other words, customers are 11.43 times more likely to buy a product p_i if i is lower than, or equal to, the index limit predicted by the Purchase Function. We refer to this ratio as $\frac{P_f(p_i, c_j)}{P(p_i, c_j)}$, i.e. the f_*-based probability of connecting customer c_j with product p_i over the baseline probability. We also calculated the same ratio, this time by counting at the right side of the isocline, where we expect to find many zeros. The number of ones is 37 millions minus 16 millions, and it is divided by the number of cells, 1.5 billions minus 60 millions. The probability of obtaining a one is 1.39%, less than one twentieth of the left side of the isocline.

Now that we have addressed the main concern about the Purchase Function, we can safely assign to product p_i a corresponding customer index $j = -\frac{\beta i + \delta}{\gamma i + \alpha}$ that is its current 'border'. All indexes $j' \leq j$ represents customers who buy product p_i (i.e. $\forall j' \leq j$, $c_{j'} \in$ customer_base(p_i)), while the indexes $j'' > j$ are customers not buying p_i. By definition, the higher the value of j'', the more unlikely is the customer buying p_i. Thus, the set

Table 6 The probabilities of buying product p_i in general ($P(p_i)$) and given that a customer already buys product p_{i-1} ($P(p_i|p_{i-1})$)

p_i	p_{i-1}	$P(p_i)$	$P(p_i|p_{i-1})$
Dishwasher salt	Dishwasher soap	8.39%	30.41%
Asparagus	Olive	8.00%	26.12%
Peppers	Chicory	7.31%	23.73%
Canned soup	Preserved anchovies	9.96%	32.23%
Wafers	Sugar candies	11.30%	21.67%

Table 7 The comparison between the size of the target customer sets identified by the Purchase Function against random target customer sets with the same number of customers likely to buy p_i

p_i	$|TC^*|$	$|TC|$	$\frac{|TC_r|}{|TC|}$
Tomino cheese	58	137	7.51095
Raw ham	78	144	5.81250
Apricot jam	66	127	4.66142
Anchovies	83	144	4.06250

of customers the law is suggesting to target is the one immediately after index j. Since f_* is an interpolation, it is safe to define a threshold ϵ_1. Then, we define the set TC, the target customers set, as the set of all customers for which, given their index j', it holds: $j - \epsilon_1 \leq j' \leq j + \epsilon_1$ and $M_{cp}(c_j, p_i) \neq 1$ (the last condition is necessary to exclude from TC all customers who are already buying large quantities of product p_i, as it is useless to advertise p_i to them).

To evaluate how many elements of TC are likely to start buying p_i, we remark that having a 1 in the product of index $i - 1$ makes the customer very likely to buy the next more sophisticated product p_i. In other words, to have purchased large amounts of the product immediately to the left in the matrix to p_i increase to probability of purchase this product. For instance, customers buying 'dishwasher soap' have 30.41% probability of buying product 'dishwasher salt' against a baseline probability of 8.39%, some instances of this are provided in Table 6. On average, the $\frac{P(p_i|p_{i-1})}{P(p_i)}$ ratio is 1.993 for the 500 most sold products, and no single product has a ratio lower than 1 (the lowest is 1.05 for Fresh Bread). Therefore, $\forall tc \in TC$ we check if $\exists x, M_{cp}(tc, p_x) = 1$, with $i - \epsilon_2 \leq x < i$, thus looking not only at the direct left neighbor of product p_i, but at his ϵ_2 left neighbors. If the condition holds, we have identified TC^* as the subset of TC composed by those customers who are likely to buy p_i.

The question now is: how large should be a TC_r set to obtain an equally large TC_r^* set if TC_r has been populated without knowledge about the Purchase Function, i.e. at random by picking customers who are not already buying product p_i? We address this question by looking at several different products. For each of them we identified the TC set using f_* and then we calculated 500 random TC_r sets. In Table 7 we report, for each product p_i, the following statistics: the number of customers likely to purchase p_i ($|TC^*|$ column), the total number of targeted customers ($|TC|$ column) and the average ratio between the targeted customers without and with using the purchase function f_* ($\frac{|TC_r|}{|TC|}$), by fixing $\epsilon_1 = 100$ and $\epsilon_2 = 2$. As we can see, the knowledge provided by the Purchase Function reduces the number of customers to be targeted by a marketing campaign by four or more times, with the same return of investment (as our procedure fixes $|TC^*| = |TC_r^*|$). Table 7 reports only a few products, but we tested these 500 random sets for 800 different products and

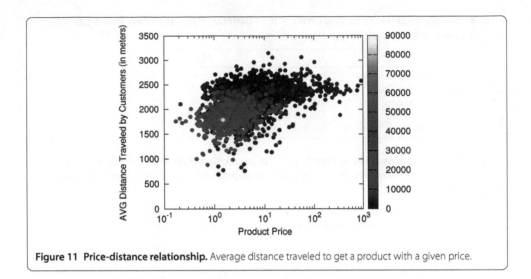

Figure 11 Price-distance relationship. Average distance traveled to get a product with a given price.

the average of the averages of the $\frac{|TC_r|}{|TC|}$ ratio is 3.55594, i.e. on average using the Purchase Function the marketing campaign can target three times less customers with the same gross return. For none of the 800 products the average of the ratio was less than 1.

4.3 Predicting customer mobility

To explain customer mobility is one of the successes of this framework. The full study of the application has been published in [21], without the framework formalization. We report here the results to prove the usefulness of this framework. Customer mobility has been shown to be rather predictable on long time scales [22]. In [22], authors show that it is possible to model the overall mobility behavior of customers. More than showing the predictability of customer movements as in [22], we focus in one of the possible causes of it.

We assume that customers modify their shopping behaviour according to their relative position to the shop they are going to. A customer may decide to buy or not buy a given product because it is close enough or too far away from the shop. We expect that customers will travel more to purchase products that are more expensive, for many possible reasons. For example, a larger money investment makes less important the amount of time spent in doing it. We check this hypothesis by plotting for each purchase the price of an item against the average distance that a customer travelled to get the product. This plot is depicted in Figure 11: the price is on the x axis (in logarithmic scale), while the distance travelled is on the y axis. The price is recorded in Euros. Each dot is a purchase and we color it accordingly to how many purchases are represented by the same price and by the same distance.

The connection of a customer to a product is created with the procedure described in the pre-process section, therefore we are only considering connections generated when the quantity of product p bought by customer c_i is significant. A customer c_i may have bought product p_j in different shops, say s_1, s_2, s_3, s_4. In this case, we weigh each distance travelled with the amount of purchases made using the following formula:

$$d(c_i, p_j) = \sum_{\forall s \in S} \frac{p_j(c_i, s) \times d(c_i, s)}{p_j(c_i, *)},$$

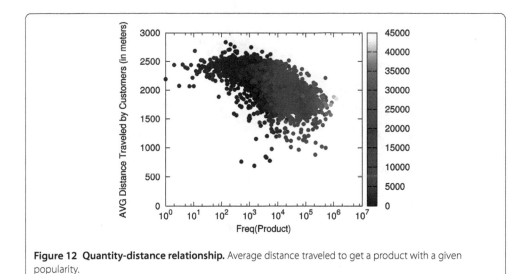

Figure 12 Quantity-distance relationship. Average distance traveled to get a product with a given popularity.

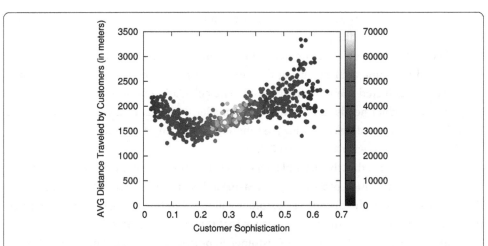

Figure 13 Product sophistication-distance relationship. Average distance traveled to get a product with a given sophistication index.

where S is the set of all shops, $d(c_i, s)$ is the distance between customer c_i and shop s, $p_j(c_i, s)$ and $p_j(c_i, *)$ are the amount of purchases of product p_j made by customer c_i in shop s and in general, respectively. This procedure has been followed for the plots depicted in Figures 11, 12, 13 and 14.

Products with the same price are bought by customers placed at different distances from the shop. Given a price, we average the distance travelled by the customers buying the products with that exact price. By averaging, we lose the ability of describing each single customer and we just describe the behaviour of the system in its entirety. We do so because the single customer is bounded by the place where she lives, thus each single customer carries a noisy information, and we can make sense of it only by looking at the global level.

From Figure 11 we can conclude that price plays a role in driving customer decisions of travelling a given distance for a product. The correlation here looks weak, but positive: customers travel more if they need to buy a more expensive product. We calculate a log-linear regression[d] using the function $f(x) = a \log x + b$. In this regression, $R^2 = 17.25\%$ ($r =$

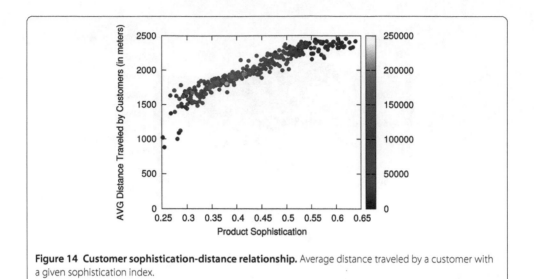

Figure 14 Customer sophistication-distance relationship. Average distance traveled by a customer with a given sophistication index.

0.4154, with p-value < 0.01), meaning that we can explain 17.25% of the variance in the distance travelled using the price.

To check if the frequency of purchase can explain the distance travelled by customers, we repeated the same analysis, using the number of purchases of a product instead of the price. We depicted the plot in Figure 12. The correlation here is negative: the more frequently a product needs to be bought, the smaller the distance a customer will travel for it. We calculate a regression with the function $f(x) = a \log x + b$ and we obtained $R^2 = 32.38\%$ ($r = -0.5691$, with p-value < 0.01).

These tests confirm that the price plays a small role in predicting the distance a customer will travel for purchasing a product, by increasing it. If a product is needed more frequently then it drives (down) the distance a customer will travel to buy it, regardless of the price. However, there is a large amount of variance that remains unexplained.

We propose that our Product and Customer Sophistication indexes have, in this case, higher explanatory power. The intuition is that if a product satisfies a more sophisticated need (and the customer has those needs) then the customer is willing to travel farther to purchase the product. To test this hypothesis, we generate the same plots created for price and frequency of purchase, using our computed indexes. The plots are depicted in Figures 13 and 14.

In Figure 13, we test the relationship between the distance travelled and the Customer Sophistication: we calculate the average distance travelled by customers (y axis) to get to the shop against their sophistication value (x axis). In this case, the x axis has not a logarithmic scale, as the relationship is linear. We can see that the relationship between distance travelled and customer sophistication looks non-linear. From a value of sophistication of 0 to around 0.2 the relationship is negative, while it is clearly positive afterwards. We speculate that this effect could be driven by the fact that customers with lower sophistication could live on average further from the shops for many reasons (they prefer living outside the city, they are in poorer areas of the city, etc.). However, to test this speculation is outside the scope of this paper and we leave it as future work.

For this reason, we move on in depicting the Product Sophistication (x axis) against the average distance travelled by the customers to purchase the given product (y axis) in Figure 14. In this case, the relationship is clear: the more a product is sophisticated, the more customers will travel to buy them. The product sophistication has a normal distribution, but less sophisticated products are more sold, given the triangular shape of the matrix. This fact explains why most of the data points are in the left part of the plot: most purchases are generated for low sophistication products. We calculated a linear regression, for which $R^2 = 85.72\%$ ($r = 0.9259$, with p-value < 0.01). This R^2 is more than twice higher than the R^2 obtained with the purchase frequency, explaining much better the variance in the distances travelled by customer.

In [21] we address possible objections such as the influence between distance and number of products bought, which may invalidate the effect of the Product Sophistication. We also show that the average Sophistication of different shop types (we recall that there are three, in decreasing order of size and Sophistication: iper, super and gestin) influence the average distance of their customers. For compactness, we point to that paper for this additional material and we conclude this section by remarking that the average sophistication of the products in a shop is influencing customers' decisions: when they need a more sophisticated product they are prone to decide to go to a larger shop with higher sophistication.

5 Discussion

In this section we firstly place this paper in the context of marketing research literature, especially in the field of data mining. We then briefly review the strong and weak points of this study. Finally, we conclude the paper, summing up contribution and future works.

5.1 Results in context with previous literature

This work is a complementary approach to the classical data mining task of the association rule mining. In data mining, association rule mining is a tool developed to find correlations between the appearances of products in shopping carts [1]. Association rule algorithms are able to uncover the most frequent and interesting rules by efficiently cutting the search space (or even without [23]). Recently, many step forwards have been proposed in association rule mining as mining multidimensional rules [24]. Our work differs from the ones presented as it is not focused on finding all the particular rules in a transactional dataset, but in exploring the general pattern characterizing it as a whole. This pattern can also be used to design better heuristics for the classical association rule mining algorithm, since it unveils novel relationships among products.

There are also works that aim to use association rule mining to obtain a general picture of the system [25]. However, also in this case our approach is different. In [25], only the associations between products are considered, leaving the customers undescribed. Then, the general picture in [25] is based on the aggregation of the local patterns, while in our work we employ a complementary approach, creating the general picture by analysing the entire set of transactions as a complex system, expressing properties at the global level that are not necessarily given by the sum of the properties at the local level. To sum up, while [25] employs a bottom-up approach, we employ a top-down approach. We employed a similar approach in previous work [26], by studying the effects of different community discovery approaches in analysing the complex network of product associations.

Other relevant literature dealing with the problem of extracting knowledge from customer behaviour can be found in business intelligence. In this field, many data mining and OLAP techniques have been developed, enriching the analytic tools [4, 27], not only for marketing purposes but also to detect frauds [28], or for public health surveillance [29]. Data mining and customer behaviour has gone also one step forward, by exploiting sentiment analysis as a prediction tool for a product success/failure [30].

Our approach is a combination of application and evolution of some tools present in literature. First, for some specific tasks our framework makes use of the Revealed Comparative Advantage (RCA) measure. The RCA measure has been defined in international economics [31], but the very same concept has been borrowed in many fields. For example, the RCA measure is equivalent to the lift. Lift (as conviction, collective strength and many more) is one criterion used in association rule mining to evaluate the interestingness of a rule [32].

Second, we make use of concepts related to ecology literature [13] and macro economics [8, 17]. While using similar techniques (as the eigenvector factorization of the customer-product matrix to calculate the sophistication levels of both customers and products), our work differs from the ones presented on two axis: quality and quantity of data. As for the quality of the data, we deal with micro purchases instead of macro world trade or ecosystem presence/absence of animal species. As for the quantity of data, we work with matrices with a number of cells $\sim 10^9$ while related works do not scale beyond $\sim 10^5$ and therefore cannot be used in our scenario.

Our analysis of customer mobility has been designed and performed also in a data-mining oriented scenario, in previous work [21]. For that paper, we also publicly released our anonymized data, for result verification purposes.[e]

5.2 Strength and limitations of this study

To the best of our knowledge, this is the first study applying the logic of complex system theory to the retail market. This is the main strength of the paper, because it empowers researchers and market analysts with a new way of thinking this field of study. Many classical results from complexity theory can now be applied to this scenario, and the universe of testable hypotheses has been enlarged.

We backed up this claim by showing three applications. We showed that it is possible to have a data-driven large scale observation of the hierarchy of human needs. Previously, this theory could only be tested in very bounded cases. Moreover, we uncovered some aspects of the logic of customer behaviour. We did so limiting our attention to their movements on the territory. As a result of our analytic vantage point, we could discover that their mobility is more predictable than previously thought. We are able to predict part of the variance in their movements just by knowing what types of products are sold in different supermarkets of an area.

There are many limitations in the study here presented. Even if we partially controlled from time and space, by creating alternative views of our dataset from different regions in space and time, we still have a biased view of customer behaviour. In fact, our entire study is confined inside the cultural environment of Italy. This makes our empirical hierarchy of needs biased towards what are the basic and sophisticated needs for the Italian people. Moreover, we used the internal marketing classification of the supermarket under study to redact our hierarchy. This is another source of bias that can be fixed by using data from other countries, as well as an international standard product classification such as SITC[f] or HS.[g]

As a second limitation, a deeper understanding of the mechanics of the purchase matrix could be a promising future work of this paper. One could define a null model using the

Maximum Entropy Principle [33] and test whether the results shown in the paper still hold.

Thirdly, in the definition of the Purchase Function, we did not consider the number of parameters as a penalty for the functional form. It is not surprise, then, that the function with more parameters fits the data better. As future work, we will include penalties for the number of parameters and test whether the current shape of the function still provides the best results.

Also the mobility study is influenced by the technology level of Italy. Countries with better, or worse, infrastructure might show different patterns.

5.3 Conclusion

In this paper we analysed large quantities of data extracted from the retail activity of the customer subset of an Italian supermarket chain. Our aim was to build a framework able to exploit a different vantage point over retail purchase data. We highlighted some properties of retail data, namely uneven distributions of connections in the customer-product bipartite structure and the triangular structure of its adjacency matrix. These properties make association rule mining results incomplete. By looking at the retail data as a complex system, as we did in this paper, we can develop an alternative and complementary methodology to analyse purchase data.

Our thesis is that customers usually buy the same set of basic products and the more sophisticated products are only bought by customers buying everything, generating a triangular adjacency matrix for the bipartite customer-product network. Our framework is able to analyse this structure as a whole, instead of looking at the local patterns like classical rule mining, uncovering the general pattern of shopping behaviour. Building on this theory, we define a the Purchase Function that can identify the set of customers buying a specific product by looking simply at how much the product is sold (and vice versa); and a way to rank the sophistication level of both products and customer needs. We showed some possible applications of these results: a data driven empirical observation of Maslow's theory of needs; an efficient way to identify a small set of potentially very interested customers for a given product p_i; and a way to predict customer mobility on the territory.

Our work opens the way to several future developments. The first one concerns the validation of our observation of the hierarchy of needs, as it is based on a narrow geographical set of people and on a non-standard product category classification. Also, with more data we can extend our pyramid of needs to fully cover the entire spectrum of human needs. Another interesting track of research may be to investigate what is the minimum time window needed to observe the prerequisites of the Purchase Function, maybe linked with the cyclic behaviour of customers [34] and/or with the stability of customer and product ranking order in the matrix [35]. Another application scenario may be to fully exploit the purchase matrix as a complex system: to analyse products not only based on their product sophistication index, but by looking at the product-product relationship level; or to try to find the way of controlling the complex system [36].

Appendix 1: Experimental setting

The analysis presented in this paper are performed with regular user-end computers. No mainframes or parallel computing techniques have been used. The fit of the Purchase

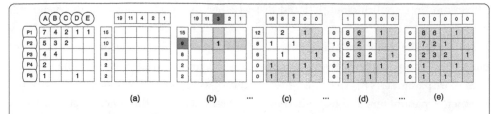

Figure 15 Null model generation. Schematic visualization of the process to generate a null model from the toy example in Figure 5. **(a)** We start from an empty matrix with a set of threshold for columns and rows; **(b)** at each step we select a pair of column and row index to increment a component; **(c)** after a sequence of assignments, the columns (rows) with no availability are blocked (grayed); **(d)** last step where only one pair of column and row is available; **(e)** the resulting null model.

Function f_*, the marketing analysis and the computing of Product and Customer Sophistication via eigenvector calculation have been performed each one in less than one hour on a Dual Core Intel i7 64 bits @ 2.8 GHz laptop, equipped with 8 GB of RAM and with a kernel Linux 3.0.0-12-generic (Ubuntu 11.10), using a combination of Octave, Numpy and Scipy Python libraries. The data preparation pipeline, and null model generation and evaluation, have been computed on a Quad Core Intel Pentium III Xeon @ 2 GHz, equipped with 8 GB of RAM and with Windows Server 2003, using Java 1.6. The most memory and time consuming operation was the null model generation: each null model required 6 GB of memory and 4 hours of computing. The conclusion is that our framework is able to scale and to analyse large data quantities.

Appendix 2: Null model

For the null model, we need to generate a random matrix where the observed sums of rows and columns are preserved. In literature there is an algorithm providing this feature [37], but it is not designed to work on very large matrices. Therefore, we extract a null model according to the algorithm explained below. A visual schematic representation of the different steps is presented in Figure 15.

We use two sets (*PLeft* and *CLeft*) to keep track of the rows and columns that are not yet full: customers that have not yet reached their amount of products bought and products that have not yet reached their diffusion among the customers. Vector R (C) keeps track in each cell of the respective residual in the row (column). The integer *NItemsLeft* contains the total number of purchases.

We start from an empty matrix, with the same dimensions as our real data matrix and with all cells initialized at 0. We iterate until we have a product left to place, i.e. as long as *NItemsLeft* > 0. At each iteration we randomly extract a position from the set of cells that are still increasable (stored in *CLeft* and *PLeft*). At this point, we just increase by 1 the value of the cell extracted, we decrease the residual of the row and the column selected (in R and P) and of the total number of purchases (*NItemsLeft*). Finally, we check if the column (row) selected has been filled and, in this case, we remove the column (row) index from the set *Pleft* (*CLeft*). After building this null adjacency matrix, we calculate the RCA for each cell, applying the pre-process step of our methodology. We obtain a null M_{cp} matrix and we can then confront it with the original one to understand if they are similar or not (and therefore if the shape of the original matrix is meaningful or not).

Competing interests

The authors declare that they have no competing interests.

Authors' contributions

DP1 and MC performed research, prepared figures, carried out empirical analysis and wrote the manuscript. All authors designed research and reviewed the manuscript.

Author details

[1]IMT, P.za San Ponziano 6, Lucca, Italy. [2]ISTI, CNR, Via G. Moruzzi, 1, Pisa, Italy. [3]CID, Harvard University, 79 JFK St, Cambridge, USA. [4]Department of Informatics, University of Pisa, Largo B. Pontecorvo 3, Pisa, Italy.

Acknowledgements

We gratefully thank Muhammed Yildirim, César Hidalgo, Jenny Zambon and Sebastian Bustos for their support and useful discussions. We thank the supermarket company Coop and Walter Fabbri for sharing the data with us and allowing us to analyse and to publish the results. This work has been partially supported by the European Commission under the FET-Open Project n. FP7-ICT-270833, DATA SIM.

Endnotes

[a] The news of the study, in Italian, can be found at http://www.viasarfatti25.unibocconi.it/notizia.php?idArt=6527. The PI of the study can be reached at isabella.soscia@skema.edu.

[b] Also note that, for some reason, 'Chemicals' such as band aids or rat poison are classified under 'Food', although we advise not to eat these things.

[c] This happens because the matrix is subject to the Perron-Frobenius theorem. To be applicable, the theorem has two requirements: the matrix must be aperiodic and irreducible. Being symmetric, $\tilde{M}$ satisfies the aperiodicity requirement. We also make use only of the largest giant component of $M_{c,p}$, which implies that $\tilde{M}$ has only one component too, and thus satisfies the irreducibility requirement.

[d] This and all other regressions have been calculated with the *leastsq* function of the *SciPy* module for Python.

[e] http://www.michelecoscia.com/?page_id=379.

[f] http://unstats.un.org/unsd/cr/registry/regcst.asp?Cl=14.

[g] http://hts.usitc.gov/.

References

1. Agrawal R, Imielinski T, Swami AN (1993) Mining association rules between sets of items in large databases. In: SIGMOD international conference, Washington, D.C., pp 207-216
2. Sun Y, Aggarwal CC, Han J (2012) Relation strength-aware clustering of heterogeneous information networks with incomplete attributes. Proc VLDB Endow 5(5):394-405
3. Chaudhuri S, Narasayya VR (2011) New frontiers in business intelligence. Proc VLDB Endow 4(12):1502-1503
4. Kocakoç ID, Erdem S (2010) Business intelligence applications in retail business: OLAP, data mining & reporting services. J Inf Knowl Manag 9(2):171-181
5. Brauckhoff D, Dimitropoulos X, Wagner A, Salamatian K (2012) Anomaly extraction in backbone networks using association rules. IEEE/ACM Trans Netw 20(6):1788-1799
6. Marinica C, Guillet F (2010) Knowledge-based interactive postmining of association rules using ontologies. IEEE Trans Knowl Data Eng 22(6):784-797
7. Montella A (2011) Identifying crash contributory factors at urban roundabouts and using association rules to explore their relationships to different crash types. Accid Anal Prev 43(4):1451-1463
8. Hidalgo CA, Klinger B, Barabási AL, Hausmann R (2007) The product space conditions the development of nations. Science 317(5837):482-487. doi:10.1126/science.1144581
9. Hausmann R, Hidalgo C, Bustos S, Coscia M, Chung S, Jimenez J, Simoes A, Yildirim M (2011) The atlas of economic complexity. Boston, USA
10. Caldarelli G, Cristelli M, Gabrielli A, Pietronero L, Scala A, Tacchella A (2011) Ranking and clustering countries and their products; a network analysis. arXiv:1108.2590
11. Davis WL, IV, Schwarz P, Terzi E (2009) Finding representative association rules from large rule collections. In: SDM, pp 521-532
12. Maslow AH (1943) A theory of human motivation. Psychol Rev 50(4):370-396
13. Bascompte J, Jordano P, Melián CJ, Olesen JM (2003) The nested assembly of plant-animal mutualistic networks. Proc Natl Acad Sci USA 100(16):9383-9387. doi:10.1073/pnas.1633576100
14. Almeida-Neto M, Guimarães P, Guimarães PR, Jr., Loyola RD, Ulrich W (2008) A consistent metric for nestedness analysis in ecological systems: reconciling concept and measurement. Oikos 117:1227-1239. doi:10.1111/j.0030-1299.2008.16644.x
15. Pennacchioli D, Coscia M, Giannotti F, Pedreschi D (2013) Calculating product and customer sophistication on a large transactional dataset. Technical report cnr.isti/2013-TR-004
16. Marquardt DW (1963) An algorithm for least-squares estimation of nonlinear parameters. J Soc Ind Appl Math 11(2):431-441
17. Hidalgo CA, Hausmann R (2009) The building blocks of economic complexity. Proc Natl Acad Sci USA 106(26):10570-10575. doi:10.1073/pnas.0900943106
18. Cristelli M, Gabrielli A, Tacchella A, Caldarelli G, Pietronero L (2013) Measuring the intangibles: a metrics for the economic complexity of countries and products. PLoS ONE 8(8):e70726
19. Guidotti R (2013) Mobility ranking - human mobility analysis using ranking measures. University of Pisa

20. Wang H, Song M (2011) Ckmeans.1d.dp: optimal k-means clustering in one dimension by dynamic programming. R J 3(2):29-33

21. Pennacchioli D, Coscia M, Rinzivillo S, Pedreschi D, Giannotti F (2013) Explaining the product range effect in purchase data. In: 2013 IEEE international conference on big data, pp 648-656

22. Krumme C, Llorente A, Cebrián M, Pentland A, Egido EM (2013) The predictability of consumer visitation patterns. CoRR. arXiv:abs/1305.1120

23. Cohen E, Datar M, Fujiwara S, Gionis A, Indyk P, Motwani R, Ullman JD, Yang C (2000) Finding interesting associations without support pruning. In: ICDE, pp 489-500

24. Nguyen K-N, Cerf L, Plantevit M, Boulicaut J-F (2011) Multidimensional association rules in Boolean tensors. In: SDM, pp 570-581

25. Chawla S (2010) Feature selection, association rules network and theory building. J Mach Learn Res 10:14-21

26. Pennacchioli D, Coscia M, Pedreschi D (2014) Overlap versus partition: marketing classification and customer profiling in complex networks of products. In: Workshop of the international conference of data engineering (ICDE)

27. Li H (2005) Applications of data warehousing and data mining in the retail industry. In: Proceedings of ICSSSM'05: 2005 international conference on services systems and services management, vol 2

28. Gabbur P, Pankanti S, Fan Q, Trinh H (2011) A pattern discovery approach to retail fraud detection. In: KDD, pp 307-315

29. Wagner MM, Robinson JM, Tsui F-C, Espino JU, Hogan WR (2003) Design of a national retail data monitor for public health surveillance. J Am Med Inform Assoc 10(5):409-418

30. Castellanos M, Dayal U, Hsu M, Ghosh R, Dekhil M, Lu Y, Zhang L, Schreiman M (2011) LCI: a social channel analysis platform for live customer intelligence. In: SIGMOD conference, pp 1049-1058

31. Balassa B (1965) Trade liberalization and 'revealed' comparative advantage. Manch Sch 33:99-123

32. Geng L, Hamilton HJ (2006) Interestingness measures for data mining: a survey. ACM Comput Surv 38(3):9. doi:10.1145/1132960.1132963

33. Bousquet N (2010) Eliciting vague but proper maximal entropy priors in Bayesian experiments. Stat Pap 51(3):613-628

34. Shen Z-JM, Su X (2007) Customer behavior modeling in revenue management and auctions: a review and new research opportunities. Prod Oper Manag 16(6):713-728. doi:10.1111/j.1937-5956.2007.tb00291.x

35. Schich M, Lehmann S, Park J (2008) Dissecting the canon: visual subject co-popularity networks in art research. In: ECCS2008

36. Liu Y-Y, Slotine J-J, Barabási A-L (2011) Controllability of complex networks. Nature 473(7346):167-173. doi:10.1038/nature10011

37. Patefield WM (1981) An efficient method of generating random RxC tables with given row and column totals (algorithm AS 159). J R Stat Soc, Ser C, Appl Stat 30:91-97. doi:10.2307/2346669

Permissions

The contributors of this book come from diverse backgrounds, making this book a truly international effort. This book will bring forth new frontiers with its revolutionizing research information and detailed analysis of the nascent developments around the world.

We would like to thank all the contributing authors for lending their expertise to make the book truly unique. They have played a crucial role in the development of this book. Without their invaluable contributions this book wouldn't have been possible. They have made vital efforts to compile up to date information on the varied aspects of this subject to make this book a valuable addition to the collection of many professionals and students.

This book was conceptualized with the vision of imparting up-to-date information and advanced data in this field. To ensure the same, a matchless editorial board was set up. Every individual on the board went through rigorous rounds of assessment to prove their worth. After which they invested a large part of their time researching and compiling the most relevant data for our readers.

The editorial board has been involved in producing this book since its inception. They have spent rigorous hours researching and exploring the diverse topics which have resulted in the successful publishing of this book. They have passed on their knowledge of decades through this book. To expedite this challenging task, the publisher supported the team at every step. A small team of assistant editors was also appointed to further simplify the editing procedure and attain best results for the readers.

Apart from the editorial board, the designing team has also invested a significant amount of their time in understanding the subject and creating the most relevant covers. They scrutinized every image to scout for the most suitable representation of the subject and create an appropriate cover for the book.

The publishing team has been an ardent support to the editorial, designing and production team. Their endless efforts to recruit the best for this project, has resulted in the accomplishment of this book. They are a veteran in the field of academics and their pool of knowledge is as vast as their experience in printing. Their expertise and guidance has proved useful at every step. Their uncompromising quality standards have made this book an exceptional effort. Their encouragement from time to time has been an inspiration for everyone.

The publisher and the editorial board hope that this book will prove to be a valuable piece of knowledge for researchers, students, practitioners and scholars across the globe.

List of Contributors

Emilio Ferrara
Center for Complex Networks and Systems Research, School of Informatics and Computing, Indiana University, Bloomington, USA Department of Mathematics and Informatics, University of Messina, Messina, Italy

Christian Schulz
Department of Humanities and Social Sciences, Chair of Sociology, in particular of Modeling and Simulation, ETH Zurich, Clausiusstrasse 50, CH-8092 Zurich, Switzerland

Amin Mazloumian
Department of Humanities and Social Sciences, Chair of Sociology, in particular of Modeling and Simulation, ETH Zurich, Clausiusstrasse 50, CH-8092 Zurich, Switzerland

Alexander M Petersen
IMT Institute for Advanced Studies Lucca, Piazza San Francesco 19, 55100 Lucca, Italy

Orion Penner
IMT Institute for Advanced Studies Lucca, Piazza San Francesco 19, 55100 Lucca, Italy

Dirk Helbing
Department of Humanities and Social Sciences, Chair of Sociology, in particular of Modeling and Simulation, ETH Zurich, Clausiusstrasse 50, CH-8092 Zurich, Switzerland

Serguei Saavedra
Integrative Ecology Group, Estación Biológica de Doñana (EBD-CSIC), Calle Américo Vespucio s/n, Sevilla, 41092, Spain

Luis J Gilarranz
Integrative Ecology Group, Estación Biológica de Doñana (EBD-CSIC), Calle Américo Vespucio s/n, Sevilla, 41092, Spain

Rudolf P Rohr
Integrative Ecology Group, Estación Biológica de Doñana (EBD-CSIC), Calle Américo Vespucio s/n, Sevilla, 41092, Spain
Unit of Ecology and Evolution, Department of Biology, University of Fribourg, Chemin du Musée 10, Fribourg, 1700, Switzerland

Michael Schnabel
Northwestern Institute on Complex Systems, Northwestern University, Evanston, Illinois 60208, USA Kellogg School of Management, Northwestern University, Evanston, Illinois 60208, USA

Brian Uzzi
Northwestern Institute on Complex Systems, Northwestern University, Evanston, Illinois 60208, USA Kellogg School of Management, Northwestern University, Evanston, Illinois 60208, USA

Jordi Bascompte
Integrative Ecology Group, Estación Biológica de Doñana (EBD-CSIC), Calle Américo Vespucio s/n, Sevilla, 41092, Spain

Anna Monreale
Department of Computer Science, University of Pisa, Largo Pontecorvo, 3, Pisa, Italy
ISTI-CNR, Via G. Moruzzi, 1, Pisa, Italy

Salvatore Rinzivillo
ISTI-CNR, Via G. Moruzzi, 1, Pisa, Italy

Francesca Pratesi
Department of Computer Science, University of Pisa, Largo Pontecorvo, 3, Pisa, Italy
ISTI-CNR, Via G. Moruzzi, 1, Pisa, Italy

Fosca Giannotti
ISTI-CNR, Via G. Moruzzi, 1, Pisa, Italy

Dino Pedreschi
Department of Computer Science, University of Pisa, Largo Pontecorvo, 3, Pisa, Italy

Paolo Bajardi
Aizoon Technology Consulting, via Po 14, Torino, 10123, Italy

Matteo Delfino
ISI Foundation, via Alassio 11/C, Torino, 10126, Italy

Andre Panisson
ISI Foundation, via Alassio 11/C, Torino, 10126, Italy

Giovanni Petri
ISI Foundation, via Alassio 11/C, Torino, 10126, Italy

Michele Tizzoni
ISI Foundation, via Alassio 11/C, Torino, 10126, Italy

Diego Pennacchioli
IMT, P.za San Ponziano 6, Lucca, Italy
ISTI, CNR, Via G.Moruzzi, 1, Pisa, Italy

Michele Coscia
CID, Harvard University, 79 JFK St, Cambridge, USA

Salvatore Rinzivillo
ISTI, CNR, Via G.Moruzzi, 1, Pisa, Italy

Fosca Giannotti
ISTI, CNR, Via G.Moruzzi, 1, Pisa, Italy

Dino Pedreschi
ISTI, CNR, Via G.Moruzzi, 1, Pisa, Italy
Department of Informatics, University of Pisa, Largo B.
Pontecorvo 3, Pisa, Italy

Printed in the USA
CPSIA information can be obtained
at www.ICGtesting.com
JSHW051447221024
72173JS00006B/1601

9 781682 850008